CLASS WAR, USA

CLASS WAR, USA

*Dispatches from
the Front Lines
of Workers' Struggles
in America*

BRANDON WEBER

Haymarket Books
Chicago, Illinois

Published in 2018 by
Haymarket Books
P.O. Box 180165
Chicago, IL 60618
773-583-7884
www.haymarketbooks.org
info@haymarketbooks.org

ISBN: 978-1-60846-847-8

Trade distribution:
In the US, Consortium Book Sales and Distribution, www.cbsd.com
In Canada, Publishers Group Canada, www.pgcbooks.ca
In the UK, Turnaround Publisher Services, www.turnaround-uk.com
All other countries, Ingram Publisher Services International,
IPS_Intlsales@ingramcontent.com

Cover design by Michel Vrana. Cover image from 1934 Minneapolis teamster strike.

This book was published with the generous support of Lannan Foundation
and Wallace Action Fund.

Printed in Canada by union labor.

Library of Congress Cataloging-in-Publication data is available.

10 9 8 7 6 5 4 3 2 1

To my wife: Nothing and nobody gives me more inspiration

To my children: My wish is that the world you come to live in will not need the kinds of struggles you see here. But if it does, I know you will grow to meet them, and you will take them on like the champions that you are

And to all of my parents, for showing me what it means to fight like hell for the world you want to live in

TABLE OF CONTENTS

FOREWORD

Brandon Weber is a fighter. He's a damn fine storyteller, too.

In this new collection of stories, Weber tells the tales of those who came before: their lives, their struggles, their fights, and their victories—victories we share in (and take for granted) to this day. His writing reads less like a historical text and more like a playbook for twenty-first-century organizing.

I think that's the point.

We're in perilous times. But there have been perilous times before. In fact, there are few, if any, struggles facing the working class of 2018 that haven't already been met head-on by the working classes of the past. And therein lies what makes this collection so special.

What did they do? How did they respond? These questions are not only answered within these slender but insightful texts but also serve as a North Star in helping us figure out what we should consider as we move forward and navigate our own treacherous shoals.

This is not a collection of mini-biographies. You won't find stories of how some individual won a victory all on their own here, gang. No, this book is about those who hit the streets, walked the picket, and did the fighting—all side by side with their sisters and brothers. I'm reminded of something written by US Civil War veteran Sam Watkins, in describing his memoir, *Co. Aytch*: "To tell of the fellows who did the shooting and killing, the fortifying and ditching, the sweeping of the streets, the drilling, the standing guard, picket and vidette, and who drew (or were to draw) eleven dollars per month and rations, and also drew the ramrod and tore the cartridge."

It's those stories Brother Weber has presented here—stories of those who've done the fighting for the working class.

This is also a story about the power of solidarity.

I won't be so cliché as to quote the late Margaret Mead, but . . . as Margaret Mead said, "Never doubt that a small group of thoughtful, committed citizens can change the world; indeed, it's the only thing that ever has."

This collection serves as a testimony to that claim.

As this volume reflects, while the cause du jour has changed from time to time, in the end, it's solidarity that has always led to positive change for humanity. It was solidarity that won women the right to vote. It was solidarity that built the labor movement. It was solidarity that drove the civil rights movement. It was solidarity that led to marriage equality. It was solidarity that ended slavery in the nineteenth century and it will be solidarity that will prevents it in the twenty-first.

I look forward to seeing you in the streets. I look forward to our shared fights and victories. I look forward to a new era of working-class fighters, giving Brother Weber good stories for his sequel.

Will Fischer

Washington, DC

February 2017

INTRODUCTION

I grew up the son of a union man, a member of UAW Local 838. My parents split when I was six, and I got to learn what it was like to live with a strong woman—a woman who wouldn't take shit from anybody.

I stayed in touch with my dad enough to know when the John Deere plant was on strike, or when the workers were locked out and times were rough, rations of 1970s-era "government cheese" and powdered milk were being utilized by many families in the area. He spent thirty-six years on the shop floor, loved pretty much every minute of it, and was an active union steward for a long time, helping to defend workers who needed an advocate along the way.

My stepmother was local president of the town textile shop.

Not five miles from our house, Rath Packing company would belch out its rather ominous odors every morning as the kill line got into action. All those workers were union members, and many of the kids I grew up with had parents who worked there or at John Deere or some other union shop in town. Generally, they all made a pretty good living and could count on a pension and health care in retirement.

Why am I listing credentials like this? Because we're in danger of losing labor unions from our landscape. With them go good wages, benefits, health care, pensions, control over work life, dignity, and so much more.

The stories I have told here are about some of the things that working people went through to make a better life for themselves and for their children and their future grandchildren. Really, that's what unions are all about: let's set some ground rules so that future workers can get a piece of that American Dream pie. I have purposefully chosen stories that capture the spirit of fighting back— even when sometimes the battles end in apparent defeat for workers and veterans.

As my friend Will says in his foreword, we've been here before; unions have been on the ropes, and the companies—the 1 percent, to use current terminology—have taken away from working people everything but the bare bones needed to survive . . . if they even left that.

We clawed our way back—the collective, down-through-the-generations "we," the folks who fought at Ludlow, and Blair Mountain, and the US Postal Service, and the Lowell mills, and on the streets, and in the halls of Washington, DC.

We will arise again . . . count on it!

July 2017

1.

JOE HILL

*Labor's Best-Known Songwriter
Refused to be Buried in the State of Utah*

I f you're a fan of folk music or words and music about working people, you're probably familiar with the song "Joe Hill."

The song, originally written as a poem by Alfred Hayes and set to music by Earl Robinson, has been performed for decades by the likes of Paul Robeson, Joan Baez (at Woodstock in 1969), Phil Ochs, and Billy Bragg. Among the more memorable renditions is a version by Bruce Springsteen.

The song's lyrics recall a dream in which Joe Hill, a hero to workers who was framed on a murder charge and sentenced to death, returns in a supernatural form, symbolizing the spirit of the labor movement.

> *I dreamed I saw Joe Hill last night*
> *Alive as you or me*
> *Says I, But Joe, you're ten years dead*
> *I never died, says he*
> *I never died, says he...*

Joe Hill was not a fictional character. He was a poet, songwriter, union activist, and hero. (He also inspired the famous union phrase "Don't mourn, organize!" More on that later.)

Born October 7, 1879, in Gävle, Sweden, and named Joel Emmanuel Hägglund, he came to the United States in 1902 with the hopes of finding work. He adapted to his new home by changing his name to Joseph Hillstrom, which he later shortened to Joe Hill once he began to write songs and organize for the rights of workers.

Upon arrival in New York City, he sought employment as a migrant laborer but found opportunities sporadic and sometimes nonexistent, and always rather brutal—especially for immigrants. This sparked his interest in labor unions, which would give him and his coworkers a voice on the job no matter where they worked.

He found his calling when he discovered the fledgling Industrial Workers of the World (IWW). One of the IWW rallying cries was "one big union," and its goal was to unite every working person worldwide into one union. That sat very well with Hill.

Having been raised in a musical family, he began writing songs, poems, and powerful speeches after joining the IWW. He became the resident lyricist and a frequent cartoonist. Hill wrote songs about different types of IWW members, from immigrant factory and railway workers to itinerant laborers moving across the country from job to job. His songs inspired people—and still do today.

His popularity grew when the IWW published the first version of its *Little Red Songbook* in 1909. The musical collection, bearing the subtitle "Songs to Fan the Flames of Discontent," was made up mostly of Hill's compositions.

It included the song "There Is Power in a Union," about . . .

Joe Hill

First Edition, *Little Red Songbook*

well, power in a union, and "The Preacher and the Slave," about how religion causes people to fight for things in heaven rather than on earth:

> You will eat, by and by
> In that glorious land above the sky
> Work and pray, live on hay
> You'll get pie in the sky when you die
> [Crowd shouts, "That's a lie!"]

(This song is, in fact, where the phrase "pie in the sky" was born.)

Hill would show up at picket lines and strikes across the country, getting the crowds energized and ready to fight. His activism drew the attention of anti-union political leaders and their lackeys, too. In June 1913, he was arrested for "vagrancy" during a dockworkers' strike in San Pedro, California, and put in jail for thirty days. The real reason for the incarceration, according to Hill, was that he "was a little too active to suit the chief of the burg."

So, Hill was on the radar of cops and politicians who didn't want to see unions establishing a presence in their towns. He may have been even more worrisome to authorities than other union leaders since he could energize the workers and reinforce their solidarity with song.

But one cold night in 1914, a turn of events made Joe Hill's name internationally known. Hill, who was in Salt Lake City to work in the mines, knocked on a doctor's door at 11:30 p.m., needing treatment for a gunshot wound to his chest. Hill told the doctor he had been shot by a rival suitor for a woman's affection—he never did tell anybody her name.

On that same night, a former police officer named John Morrison and one of his sons were killed in the grocery store owned by

Cover of "The Rebel Girl" by Joe Hill. First published in *The Little Red Songbook*, it was released as sheet music in 1915.

Morrison. The murders appeared to be motivated by revenge, perhaps a holdover from Morrison's previous career in law enforcement, as the store was not robbed. Another of Morrison's sons witnessed the shooting and stated that one of the two killers shouted, "We've got you now!" before pulling the trigger.

(And just to note: at least four other people were shot in Salt Lake City that night.)

The doctor who tended to Hill's injuries noted that it was a gunshot to the chest—the same kind as the shopkeeper's surviving son said had occurred with the intruder who killed his father and brother. Over the next few days, twelve different men were arrested for the killings—and each, in succession, was released. Around the time that the twelfth man was cleared, the doctor came forward and offered his patient as a possible suspect. Hill was arrested.

When the grocer's surviving son saw Joe, he stated, "That's not him at all!" However, a few days later, after the publicity started and authorities knew they had the famous Joe Hill, he changed his mind and claimed it was definitely Hill he had seen that night.

Several aspects of the case made Hill an unlikely suspect. His injury, a shot through the left lung, would have bled profusely. Yet authorities did not find any blood in the store other than the victims'. No bullet was ever found, nor was there a motive; Joe did not know the shopkeeper, and the assailants didn't even take the money in the register.

The trial itself was a poor excuse for justice, according to author William Adler. Although two young, unknown attorneys volunteered to defend Hill, it became clear partway through that they weren't doing anything of the sort. Hill requested new lawyers, but the judge refused. From that point on, Hill refused to participate in the trial and remained silent.

(In a letter written in 1949, the woman who was there when Hill was shot, Hilda Erickson, confessed that it was her former fiancé and a friend of Joe Hill's, Otto Appelquist, who shot him that fateful night.)

After just a few hours, the jury found the thirty-five-year-old Hill guilty. He spent twenty-two months in prison while he awaited appeals of his sentence: execution by firing squad.

The IWW sought help from other labor unions around the world, and support began to build. Backers, demanding Hill's release and a retrial, sent tens of thousands of letters and circulated petitions to influence the courts and the system. Among those advocates were then president Woodrow Wilson, the Swedish minister to the United States, thirty thousand Australian IWW members, American Federation of Labor president Samuel Gompers, and trade unions from across the world. In fact, even Helen Keller, the famed deaf and blind activist (who also belonged to the IWW), wrote to the president on Hill's behalf.

The efforts targeted Utah governor William Spry, who had been elected to office on a platform that stated he would "sweep out lawless elements, whether they be corrupt businessmen or IWW agitators." Unsurprisingly, he did not intercede on Hill's behalf.

The governor's record was clear: he had broken a large mineworkers' strike and helped the Utah Copper Company bring in strikebreakers who used hired thugs to defeat the union there. Not surprisingly, this did not help Hill one bit.

While in prison, Hill kept writing poetry, music, letters, and more. In a August 15, 1915, letter to the weekly socialist newsletter *Appeal to Reason*, he stated:

> The main and only fact worth considering, however, is

Salt Lake City Main Street, 1890. (Charles Roscoe Savage)

this: I never killed Morrison and do not know a thing about it. He was, as the records plainly show, killed by some enemy for the sake of revenge, and I have not been in the city long enough to make an enemy.

Shortly before my arrest I came down from Park City; where I was working in the mines. Owing to the prominence of Mr. Morrison, there had to be a "goat" and the undersigned being, as they thought, a friendless tramp, a Swede, and worst of all, an IWW, had no right to live anyway, and was therefore duly selected to be "the goat."

I have always worked hard for a living and paid for everything I got, and in my spare time I spend by painting pictures, writing songs and composing music.

Now, if the people of the state of Utah want to shoot me without giving me half a chance to state my side of the case, bring on your firing squads—I am ready for you. I have lived like an artist and I shall die like an artist.

In one of his last letters, to IWW founding member and leader William Dudley Haywood (better known as "Big Bill" Haywood), Hill wrote these practical yet poignant words: "Goodbye Bill. I die like a true blue rebel. Don't waste any time in mourning. Organize. . . . Could you arrange to have my body hauled to the state line to be buried? I don't want to be found dead in Utah."

Haywood changed that to the phrase that has been used by union activists ever since: "Don't mourn—organize!"

The memory of Joe Hill's words lives on in the hearts of working people the world over. Hill died on November 19, 1915. According to author Philip Sheldon Foner, when the firing squad was instructed, "Ready . . . aim, . . . " Joe Hill himself

The doctor who tended to Hill's injuries noted that it was a gunshot to the chest—the same kind as the shopkeeper's surviving son said occurred with the intruder who killed his father and brother.

issued the final order, before the commander: "Yes, aim! Let 'er go. Fire!"

Thirty thousand people came to his funeral in Chicago. Eulogies were translated into ten languages. The mourners sang songs by Hill and shut down traffic for hours as the funeral procession stretched for miles. Many had IWW patches, pennants, and red ribbons with the words, "Joe Hill, murdered by the authorities of the state of Utah, November the 19th, 1915."

Especially in times like these, when labor unions in the United States are very much on the ropes, it's good to remember the words from "I Dreamed I Saw Joe Hill Last Night," also known simply as "Joe Hill"—"I never died, says he. I never died, says he."

I dreamed I saw Joe Hill last night
Alive as you or me
Says I, But Joe, you're ten years dead
I never died, says he
I never died, says he

In Salt Lake, Joe, says I to him
Him standing by my bed
They framed you on a murder charge
Says Joe, But I ain't dead
Says Joe, But I ain't dead

The copper bosses killed you, Joe
They shot you, Joe, says I
Takes more than guns to kill a man
Says Joe, I didn't die
Says Joe, I didn't die

And standing there as big as life
And smiling with his eyes
Joe says, What they forgot to kill
Went on to organize
Went on to organize

Joe Hill ain't dead, he says to me
Joe Hill ain't never died
Where working men are out on strike
Joe Hill is at their side
Joe Hill is at their side

From San Diego up to Maine
In every mine and mill
Where workers strike and organize
Says he, You'll find Joe Hill
Says he, You'll find Joe Hill

I dreamed I saw Joe Hill last night
Alive as you or me
Says I, But Joe, you're ten years dead
I never died, says he
I never died, says he

Logo, Industrial Workers of the World

REFERENCES

Adler, William M. "The Railroading of Joe Hill." *Los Angeles Times*, November 20, 2011. http://articles.latimes.com/2011/nov/20/opinion /la-oe-adler-joehill-20111120.

AFL-CIO. "Joe Hill." Key People in Labor History. http://www.aflcio.org /About/Our-History/Key-People-in-Labor-History/Joe-Hill -1879-1915.

Baez, Joan. "Joe Hill." YouTube, July 9, 2010. https://www.youtube.com /watch?v=PX7M9psH0rM.

Foner, Philip S. *The Case of Joe Hill*. New York: International Publishers, 1965.

Greenhouse, Stephen. "Examining a Labor Hero's Death." *New York Times*, August 26, 2011. http://www.nytimes.com/2011/08/27/us/27hill.html?_r=0.

H2G2. "Joe Hill—Murderer or Martyr?" Last modified March 13, 2009. http://h2g2.com/edited_entry/A676361.

Koerner, Brendan. "Where Does the Phrase 'Pie in The Sky' Come From?" *Slate*, January 15, 2003. http://www.slate.com/articles/news_and _politics/explainer/2003/01/where_does_the_phrase_pie_in_the_sky _come_from.html.

Robeson, Paul. "Joe Hill." YouTube, July 22, 2009. https://www.youtube.com /watch?v=n8Kxq9uFDes.

Smith, Gibbs M. *Joe Hill*. Salt Lake City: Peregrine Smith Books, 1984.

Snow, Richard. "American Characters: Joe Hill." *American Heritage* 27, no. 6 (October 1976). http://www.americanheritage.com/content/joe-hill.

Springsteen, Bruce. "Joe Hill." YouTube, May 1, 2014. https://youtube.com /watch?v=T2UF8yw89yE.

Zinn, Howard. *A People's History of the United States*. New York: Harper Perennial Modern Classics, 2005.

2.

LOWELL, MASSACHUSETTS

America's Very First Union of Working Women

In Lowell, Massachusetts, way back in the 1820s, some enterprising capitalists named Waltham and Lowell figured out that they could recreate the water-powered looms they'd studied in England to turn cotton into cloth, and to create yarn as well. Setting up a series of mills—machines that did all of these things quickly and efficiently—would mean producing their bundles of yarn and cloth at a very high speed and in large quantities. As cotton production increased in the United States at an almost exponential rate in the slave-laboring South, this system would be a precursor—and a model, for that matter—for manufacturing on a mass scale that would define the Industrial Revolution.

In this "planned community," the mill machines and factories would be right next to each other, and boarding houses would be just steps away. The power for the mill—water—was a river, located right next to the buildings, and it would be harnessed to make the machines go.

The Boston Manufacturing Company was the name of the company formed in Lowell, and its owners planned the entire working community from start to finish: the machines, the work, the living quarters, the laborers, and everything else as well, including Sunday religious services. Then, they built the entire thing and got to business.

Since milling was considered "women's work," that is who was recruited—young women and

General view of spinning room, Cornell Mill, Fall River, Massachusetts, January 1912

girls from surrounding farms who needed work. There was the added bonus for management that they were more pliant and less likely to rebel against the grueling working conditions and pace; these women had not worked outside the farm before this, so it was a new experience for all.

They lived in the boarding houses next to the factories and worked twelve- and fourteen-hour days during the week and a half-day on Saturday. Living and working in close proximity to other "mill girls"—even sleeping two to a bed—meant they formed close bonds, which would be crucial when times got tough. They also formed reading circles, and spent time writing fiction and poetry and letters to home.

Of course, there were times when the mill owners and "overseers" (managers) wanted to increase profit—or perhaps the market took a downturn, and their supplies weren't in such high demand—so wages were lowered. Or they'd expect the "mill girls" to produce at ever higher rates, for no increase in pay, to meet a short-term surge in demand.

Life for mill workers was frequently hard, and the changes in wages and work expectations sometimes became a turning point for these women. It hit one such point in 1834, when the women and young girls in Lowell walked off the job because their wages were being cut. Between 1,200 and 1,500 mill women "turned out."

They headed to other, similar mills to try and encourage the workers to walk out as well. They held a rally where they signed a petition stating, "That we will not go back into the mills to work unless our wages are continued" (not lowered, in other words). Also, "That none of us will go back unless we are all receive [*sic*] as one."

Some of the Lowell "mill girls"

The mill girls experienced a sense of solidarity about their purpose, and it felt like they could succeed. The mill owners, however, were horrified (and probably terrified, too) and wanted them to cease with their "spirit of evil omen." They went back soon enough, though on the company's terms.

In 1836, a similar strike occurred, this time with slightly better results. It was clear, however, that they needed the support of the community and people in political power.

They began campaigning for a ten-hour day via letters to newspapers and to politicians about their working conditions. From 1840 to 1845, the Lowell girls even produced their own monthly magazine of poetry and fiction, *The Lowell Offering*, which humanized them to outsiders and solidified their ranks.

They organized chapters in other mill towns in Massachusetts and New Hampshire. They published "factory tracts" to expose the worst of the mills to the public and to potential new hires. Though as women they could not vote, the workers testified before a state legislative committee about their horrid working conditions. They even campaigned against and soundly defeated a state representative who was one of their staunchest enemies.

The Lowell mill workers were an inspiration to future generations of working women—and men, for that matter—who were simply not going to take it anymore.

REFERENCES

Dublin, Thomas. *Women at Work: The Transformation of Work and Community in Lowell, Massachusetts, 1826–1860*. New York: Columbia University Press, 1979.

Robinson, Harriet Hanson. "The Lowell Mill Girls Go on Strike, 1836." History Matters: George Mason University. http://historymatters.gmu.edu/d/5714.

Starkman, Dean, Martha M. Hamilton, and Ryan Chittum. *The Best Business Writing 2014*. New York: Columbia University Press, 2014.

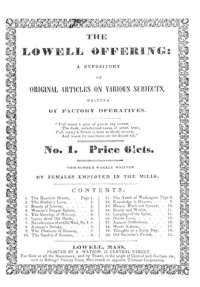

The Lowell Offering

3.

THE ATLANTA WASHERWOMEN'S STRIKE

*African American Women with the Power
to Call a General Strike—in 1881*

About twenty years after the "official" end of slavery in the United States, the country entered a period known officially as Reconstruction. However, a severe backlash against freedom for formerly enslaved African Americans arrived in the form of restrictive "Jim Crow" laws, enacted in response to the Populist movement of the 1890s, which had united Blacks and whites. Jim Crow laws mandated separate restrooms, drinking fountains, treatment by some labor unions, military units, and education at elementary schools, high schools, and colleges. In the case of education, sometimes there were simply no opportunities at all.

Lynchings were the preferred method of intimidating African Americans, especially in the South. From 1890 to 1899, for example, an average of 175 lynchings of African Americans occurred per year in the United States. (Those are the official reports; the number in reality is likely much higher.)

In this atmosphere, a group of African American women in and around Atlanta fought against everything and all odds, and struck.

The 1881 Atlanta washerwomen's strike stands as an example of what it's like when people who've been against the wall in nearly every way imaginable fight back and change things for decades—if not permanently.

At the time, 98 percent of the African American women who worked did so as household workers, and more than half of those were laundresses. Since most white households could afford a laundress (and it was usually one of the first duties they would think of paying someone else to do), there were thousands of washerwomen. Wages ranged from four to eight dollars a month, and that usually included making their own soap, starch, and washtubs. The job also included making rounds to the houses of their clients to collect the bundles of cotton garments, hauling water from the well, hanging and un-hanging items from clotheslines, pressing the clothing with large irons, and more. It was a seven-day-a-week job.

In July 1881, the Washing Society was formed—the kernel of the much larger force that would quickly develop. A strike was called to demand higher wages and better treatment, and the women canvassed neighborhoods all over the city as well as churches, seeking support from their fellow laundresses and from families and friends. The Washing Society even managed to get the 2 percent of washerwomen who were white to join. They had a few demands, including a rate of $1 per twelve pounds of laundry, as well as some autonomy over their work and more respect from clients.

In three weeks, the Washing Society—and the strike—was at three thousand members. There was the inevitable pushback from white businesses and politicians, who threatened fines, arrested some members, and otherwise tried to quell this rebellion—especially because people in other service industries were threatening the same thing.

In a move that further solidified the ranks of the strikers, the city council proposed that a washer's license—to even be able to

Francisco Laso, *The Laundress*, **1858**

Unknown artist, *Washer Woman*

wash clothes for a living—be imposed at a cost of $25. In response, the Society composed a letter that effectively said, "Bring it!"

LETTER TO MR. JAMES ENGLISH

3 August 1881
Mr. Jim English, Mayor of Atlanta
Atlanta Georgia, August 1 [1881]

Dear Sir:

We the members of our society, are determined to stand to our pledge and make extra charges for washing, and we have agreed, and are willing to pay $25 or $50 for licenses as a protection, so we can control the washing for the city. We can afford to pay these licenses, and will do it before we will be defeated, and then we will have full control of the city's washing at our own prices, as the city has control of our husbands' work at their prices. Don't forget this. We hope to hear from your council Tuesday morning. We mean business this week or no washing.

Yours respectfully,
    From 5 Societies, 486 Members

The city buckled, did not impose the fees, and the legend of the Atlanta washerwomen's strike of 1881 was born.

REFERENCES

AFL-CIO. "Atlanta's Washerwomen Strike." http://www.aflcio.org/About/Our-History/Key-Events-in-Labor-History/Atlanta-s-Washerwomen-Strike.

"African-American Laundry Women Go on Strike in Atlanta." HERB: Resources for Teachers. https://herb.ashp.cuny.edu/items/show/897.

American Social History Project/Center for Media and Learning. "Bar Graph of Lynchings of African Americans, 1890–1929." HERB: Resources for Teachers. https://herb.ashp.cuny.edu/items/show/1884.

4.

PULLMAN

*Former Slaves Were Hired to Staff Pullman Box Cars
Because They "Knew How to Be Servile."
So They Formed a Union*

THE COMPANY

One of the most well-known capitalists and entrepreneurs during a time of very few rights for workers and extreme inequality between the classes was George Pullman. His niche was the manufacture of sleeping cars for the newly expanding post–Civil War railroad system that was transporting people to various places around the country on a much more frequent basis. Pullman had an idea of improving that system with luxury sleeping cars so rail travel would be much easier and more pleasant for customers. It worked, and he added multiple layers of service over the next few decades, including gourmet meals, ultra-clean and luxurious train cars, and opulent furnishings. Most important to these new cars was the very professional staff that was key to making the travelers feel pampered.

Sleeping cars existed before Pullman, but he turned them into an extravagant mode of travel that the newly emerging middle class and the wealthy wanted to experience. He made his first luxury car around the end of the Civil War, in 1865—in fact, the very first Pullman train car was the one that brought Abraham Lincoln's body home to Illinois from Washington. It was brilliant advertising, and

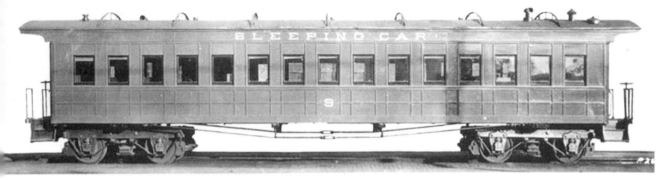

Pullman sleeping car, 1924

it worked, because it was seen by the millions who clamored to see Lincoln's body. Orders piled up overnight from train companies.

THE WORKERS

The service was one of the key features of Pullman train cars. Pullman hired thousands of former slaves, specifically for their experience of "serving" masters and their families, which then translated to the clientele on the train cars. There was a strict divide among the labor: white conductors collected tickets and sold upgrades along the routes while African American porters carried luggage, cleaned the cars, shined shoes, cooked and served meals, and made travelers feel pampered. In addition to the labor divide was one of wages—white workers received, on average, six times as much as the porters, which meant the porters relied heavily on tips.

Meanwhile, next to the factory that made these luxury train cars in Chicago, Pullman built housing, grocery stores, and just about everything else his workers would want. It sounds convenient, right? But company towns like this were prime opportunities for Pullman to take advantage of workers by raising prices and rents at will, punishing and evicting anybody who dared try to improve conditions or wages, and more. He prohibited independent newspapers and public speeches by the residents. His staff regularly inspected the workers' housing to make sure that it was clean, and he could evict anybody with a few days' notice.

All of this, plus a wage reduction with longer work hours after the 1893 depression hit, resulted in a massive strike in 1894 that was finally ended by federal troops, ordered by president Grover Cleveland. (See chapter 5).

HEY, PORTER

The real profit for Pullman was in filling the rail cars and providing a high-end service that people would pay for. Pullman sleeping cars expanded to even more markets. At its peak in the 1920s, there were twenty thousand porters on the job—the most African Americans employed by a single company in US history. There were a few women working on these trains as well; about one maid for every fifty porters was an African American woman.

One of the few well-paying jobs for African American men at the time, being a porter was a treasured position. But the work was grueling: four hundred hours a month on the job or eleven thousand miles of travel were the minimum to get full-time pay. Basically, they lived on the trains—for around $22,000 a year in today's dollars, supplemented by tips. They paid for their own clothing and lodging on layovers, and if any of the passengers made off with pillows or blankets, the cost was taken from their pay.

Work hours were one of the biggest problems. When the porters slept, it was on couches in the smoking car, hidden from the passengers. In other words, they couldn't even use the sleeping cars when they got their average of three hours of sleep per night.

Porter helping women to board the train, 1920

A Pullman porter based in Chicago

Additionally, it was a common practice for the porters to be called either "George" or a commonly used racial slur that begins with the letter "N." Effectively, "George" meant the same thing.

From 1909 to 1913, porters tried unsuccessfully to unionize three times to address some of these issues. In response, the company began its own union, which was, of course, a sham. But it distracted the efforts of workers long enough that it delayed further efforts at unionizing for another twelve years.

In 1925, the fledgling workers' union elected A. Philip Randolph to head up the unionizing drive. He was a highly skilled labor and community organizer but had never been a porter. He hadn't even ridden on a luxury train car because African Americans were not allowed to ride on the very cars that the porters serviced.

Pullman advertising poster, 1894

THE BROTHERHOOD OF SLEEPING CAR PORTERS

As soon as the union was formed, it put together a list of demands of the Pullman company:

1. A significant pay raise

2. Abolishing the practice of tipping

3. Adequate rest breaks

4. Increasing pensions

5. A name card in each car with the actual name of the porter

Since tips would often amount to more than actual wages, it seems counterintuitive that they would want to abolish tipping, right? But in reality, to get those tips, workers had to be subservient and rigidly obedient to the white clientele. Removing tips and raising wages would effectively eliminate one of the more humiliating parts of their job.

Of course, the company refused and began firing and spying on the organizers and union sympathizers. Everything had to go underground, facilitated by secret handshakes and passwords. A ladies' auxiliary unit composed of the wives of porters was formed, which was arguably one of the most critical components of the secret operations. One thing working in the porters' favor was that trains going from city to city across the country provided great opportunities for the distribution of literature, news, job information, and more.

It took twelve years for the porters to succeed. One key to victory was the 1935 passage of the National Labor Relations Act (with some pressure from president Franklin Delano Roosevelt), which gave unions legal legs when it came to organizing and prevented some of the intimidation tactics used by companies' to keep unions from forming. The first negotiating session between the company and the union was in 1935. That same year, the Brotherhood of Sleeping Car Porters became the first African American union recognized by the American Federation of Labor (AFL). The union signed its first contract with Pullman in August 1937.

The Brotherhood of Sleeping Car Porters, fresh off a significant victory, went on to help integrate other jobs and unions across the country.

REFERENCES

A. Philip Randolph Pullman Porter Museum. "Union History." https://aprpullmanportermuseum.org/about-museum /union-history/2/.

The Abraham Lincoln Pullman Car. "History of the Abraham Lincoln." http://www.pullman-car.com/history/History.html.

Chicago History Museum. "Pullman Porters, Chicago 1920s." http://facingfreedom.org/workers-rights/pullman-porters.

Harris, William, ed. *Records of the Brotherhood of Sleeping Car Porters*. Bethesda, MD: University Publications of America, 1994.

Northern Illinois University Library. "The Pullman Strike." Illinois During the Gilded Age. http://gildedage.lib.niu .edu/pullman.

Novak, Matt. "Blood on the Tracks in Pullman: Chicagoland's Failed Capitalist Utopia." *Paleofuture* (Blog), *Gizmodo*, November 13, 2014. http://paleofuture.gizmodo.com/blood-on-the-tracks-in-pullman-chicagolands-failed -cap-1574508996.

Pullman Museum. "The Pullman Company." http://www.pullman-museum.org/theCompany/.

Suzuki, Jeff. *Mathematics in Historical Context*. Washington, DC: Mathematical Association of America, 2009.

Wormser, Richard. "Brotherhood of Sleeping Car Porters." PBS: The Rise and Fall of Jim Crow. http://www.pbs.org /wnet/jimcrow/stories_org_brother.html.

5.

CHICAGO

The Haymarket Massacre of 1886 and the Pullman Strike of 1894: Chicago Was the Center of Both Struggles, and Things Got White-Hot

Two of the defining struggles near Chicago were the Haymarket Massacre of 1886 and the Pullman Strike of 1894.

PART I: THE HAYMARKET MASSACRE

There are times in our history when a massive miscarriage of justice turns lives upside down. That's what occurred at Haymarket, and it's a terrifying reminder that innocent people can be made into the guilty in a very short amount of time, and the sweeping current of mob justice cares not about truth and facts, only bloodlust.

On May 1, 1886, a rally was planned to demand an eight-hour workday, something the US labor movement had been organizing around for decades. The activists who organized the event belonged to the Knights of Labor, some anarchist groups, and other collectives and union entities,

The explosion at Haymarket Square, as interpreted by *Harper's Weekly*

and many were editors of newspapers that countered the narrative spewed by the mainstream press, which was decidedly anti-worker and pro-business.

The day came, and general strikes broke out all over the United States—ten thousand workers out in Detroit, a similar number in New York City and Milwaukee, and about forty thousand on strike in Chicago, which was the hub of the actions. Another forty thousand supporters and members of their families made the entire event eighty thousand strong in Chicago.

On the heels of that success, two days later—May 3, 1886—some of the same demonstrators showed up at a local plant, McCormick Reaper Works, where strikebreakers were being ushered in by Pinkerton guards and four hundred police. As a shift change occurred and the scab workers left the plant, there was a surge by the union members who were locked out. Police panicked (or perhaps this part was planned all along) and shot into the crowd; at least two of the workers were killed.

Some of the leadership suspected that this whole incident was purposeful, because creating violence was a quick way to shut down the eight-hour-day movement and turn public opinion against it.

A rally was scheduled for May 4 in Haymarket Square, at which several local labor and anarchist leaders were asked to speak. It was not nearly as well attended as the May 1 event, probably because people were afraid of additional violence—and that would have been smart of them.

By accounts of people who were in attendance, the speeches were peaceful, focused, and definitely not inciting anything violent. The mayor went home early because it seemed like things were going to be quiet. Several on-duty police hung around the edges of the rally and watched, not really engaged and passing time.

As the event wound down, the police moved forward, attempting to silence the final speaker as he was about to finish, pushing the crowd to disperse. Someone threw a metal-encased dynamite bomb into the advancing crowd of police and it detonated; six police were killed from that explosion alone.

As the crowd dispersed, police began firing on the fleeing demonstrators, killing at least four and wounding seventy. Sixty policemen were also wounded, although it appears that many of those injuries were from each other's revolvers.

The news media absolutely had a field day, accusing anarchists and union activists alike of attacking the police. The police proceeded to ransack the offices of the activists' respective newspapers, trying to find anything related to the bombing.

Akin to other "red scare" buildups to a political lynching that have happened throughout history, eight people were eventually selected as the "perpetrators." Of course, most were well-known union activists, anarchists with strong political views, and the like—and most were also editors and publishers of newspapers that were not part of the mainstream Chicago corporate media.

It was also a witch-hunt of immigrants; five of the eight accused were German immigrants, one was of German descent, and two were of British heritage. The most likely perpetrator

"No single event has influenced the history of labor in Illinois, the United States, and even the world, more than the Chicago Haymarket Affair. It began with a rally on May 4, 1886, but the consequences are still being felt today. Although the rally is included in American history textbooks, very few present the event accurately or point out its significance."
—William J. Adelman

of the bombing, Rudolph Schnaubelt, was arrested twice, then he fled the country before police decided he was one of the main suspects.

KANGAROO COURT AND MARTYRDOM

In every sense of the term, the trial in August was a kangaroo court; jurors were hand picked by one of the bailiffs, who was already prejudiced against the defendants. The trial was surrounded by negative press about the union activists and anarchists, using phrases such as "bloody monsters," "red ruffians," and "arch counselors of riot, pillage, incendiarism and murder." The trial quickly ended with guilty verdicts and the sentences: seven would die by hanging, and one would serve fifteen years. Protests were held around the word by labor union activists and supporters, and the defendants rapidly ascended to martyrs. Still today, when talking of Haymarket, many refer to them that way.

Appeals were filed and processed. In the end, two had their sentences commuted to life in prison, one died in prison by his own hand, and on November 11, 1887, August Spies, George Engel, Adolph Fischer, and Albert Parsons were hanged. Just before his life was ended, August Spies was able to shout out, "The time will come when our silence will be more powerful than the voices you strangle today."

It's worth noting that nobody was ever accused of making or throwing the bomb that day; these men were murdered by the state of Illinois for being active in their unions, publishing words and thoughts that were counter to the powers that be in Chicago, and associating with each other.

Far from dampening the spirit of union activists in Chicago, the Haymarket massacre unified many disparate elements of organized labor for years to come, and the first annual May Day celebration, held May 1, 1890, as a celebration of working people and a remembrance of the martyrs of Haymarket, was a success. Many to this day still celebrate May 1 as the "real" labor day, International Workers' Day.

REFERENCES

Adelman, William J. "The Haymarket Affair." Illinois Labor History Society. http://www.illinoislaborhistory.org/the-haymarket-affair/.

Library of Congress. "Topics in Chronicling America—The Haymarket Affair." https://www.loc.gov/rr/news/topics/haymarket.html.

PBS. "American Experience—People and Events: The Anarchists and the Haymarket Square Incident (May 4, 1886)." https://archive.org/details/Haymarket-Documentary.

Sismondo, Christine. *America Walks into a Bar: A Spirited History of Taverns and Saloons, Speakeasies and Grog Shops.* Oxford: Oxford University Press, 2014.

WTTW/PBS Chicago. "Haymarket Riot." http://video.wttw.com/video/1907816603/.

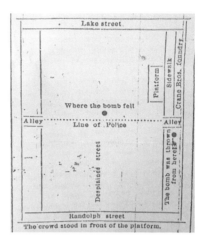

Map showing where the bomb was thrown

Coin with bomb fragment, produced by the city of Chicago. Very few are known to exist. From the private collection of Davey MacBain

Pullman strikers outside the Arcade building, state militia (National Guard) in front of the building

PART II: THE PULLMAN STRIKE

George Pullman was, by all accounts, the kind of capitalist who was widely hated by his employees, his staff, and even some fellow capitalists and government officials. He owned an area of Chicago known as the Pullman designated community area or districts, where he built his factories as well as company towns. People who worked in the Pullman Palace Car Company factory building train cars (dining cars, parlor cars, and sleeping cars—see chapter 4) lived in the company town, bought groceries from the company stores, and paid whatever Pullman decided were appropriate prices for the lot.

In 1893 a recession killed a number of businesses across the country, lowered wages across the board, and did the same to the demand for things like rail cars. Pullman thereby laid off a number of workers and lowered wages in the factories, but did not lower their rents. This incensed everyone who had to work and live there.

Enter Eugene V. Debs. With experience in the Brotherhood of Locomotive Firemen union, Debs had formed the American Railway Union (ARU) the year before, geared toward an unskilled workforce—which matched up perfectly to the workforce in Pullman's factories. The ARU quickly maneuvered into position to organize those angry workers and begin pushing back. The workers' numerous complaints included sixteen-hour workdays, a lack of democracy in Pullman's towns, the inability to purchase their own houses, paternalistic control by Pullman's management, and excessive water and gas rates—in addition to the initial grievance of lower wages without reduced rents. Pullman would not recognize the union or bargain over anything.

Rebuffed, Debs tried to take the workers at Pullman's factories out on strike. It was not getting far, so his organizers, some of the workers, and Debs himself decided that the priority needed to be this: boycott all trains that had even one Pullman car attached.

With that, everything ground to a halt. Most rail lines west of Detroit were affected, and at its peak, the boycott involved 250,000 workers in twenty-seven states, some on strike, some who participated in halting rail traffic, and some who rioted. It locked up rail systems for thousands for miles. This was a remarkable achievement, because the fledgling union was a relative unknown, and "official" unions of the time, as well as the General Managers Association of the railroads, all opposed the boycott. But several unions, notably in the rail sector, joined in.

There was palpable anger among the workers in all locations. Knowing what that could turn into in the wrong hands (and what violence would mean for public opinion), Debs was madly sending telegrams to all ARU affiliates (by some estimates, hundreds per day), asking them to remain calm.

That eventually failed, however; on June 29, after Debs spoke to a crowd in Blue Island, Illinois, and headed to his next rally, the crowd turned into a mob, which set fire to nearby buildings and then derailed a locomotive nearby.

And that was the beginning of the end. The train with the derailed locomotive included a mail car, and President Grover Cleveland saw it as one of his main jobs to keep the mail safe and moving (as most presidents do, of course—including President Nixon, who faced a much more dire interruption of the mail eighty years later; see chapter 20).

From there, the boycott fell apart quickly; antiunion judges, federal courts, governors, and the US attorney general all lined up to send in militia and federal troops, and injunctions were issued that prevented the ARU from communicating with other members. Debs's efforts to keep the peace by telegraph could not even be sent out anymore.

So you had angry strikers, the full support of several unions out in the rail yards, and the feds trying to quash all of it. Hmmm . . . what could possibly happen next?

The strikers and their supporters resorted to overturning railcars to stop troops from reaching the trains to allow them through; on July 6, it got so out of hand that hundreds of railcars were destroyed. The day of the worst violence against the strikers by the militia was July 7, 1894. When federal troops moved in, the powder keg blew once more, and gunfire rang out; dozens of strikers were killed and many wounded.

Debs tried to call off the strike at this point and have all men who hadn't committed a crime go back to work, but railroad management was having none of it. They resumed hiring replacement workers. The strike was broken, and public sentiment had strongly shifted against the ARU.

Debs was sentenced to six months in prison, where he read a lot of Karl Marx (see chapter 9). Five other ARU leaders also served time.

After things cooled, President Cleveland's administration took the time to study what happened. Upon finding that Pullman's operation was "un-American," the administration divested him of the property where his factories, houses, and company stores stood, giving them back to the city of Chicago.

A final, rather fascinating note: George Pullman was so reviled by the people who worked for him that, upon his death, his family gave specific instructions for him to be entombed in concrete and steel so that workers wouldn't defile his body.

American Railway Union membership card. Image from the private collection of Davey MacBain

REFERENCES

Bount, Pauline. "Pullman, Illinois Workers Strike for Pay (Pullman Strike), 1894." Swarthmore College: Global Nonviolent Action Database. Updated November 8, 2011. http://nvdatabase.swarthmore.edu/content/pullman-illinois-workers-strike-pay-pullman-strike-1894.

Chicago Tribune, "George Pullman's Town at Center of Labor, African-American History," February 10, 2015, http://www.chicagotribune.com/news/history/ct-pullman-history-met-20150210-story.html.

Pittman, Barbara L. "The Pullman Strike: American Railroad Crisis of 1894." American Labor Crises. Updated September 5, 2012. https://sites.google.com/site/americanlaborcrises/labor-crises/pullman-strike.

Urofsky, Melvin I. "Pullman Strike." United States History: Encyclopedia Britannica. November 18, 2014. https://www.britannica.com/event/Pullman-Strike.

On July 7, 1894, hundreds of boxcars and coal cars were looted and burned. State and federal troops were called out to stop the violence.

The American Railway Union escalated the Pullman Strike by blockading the Grand Crossing—Chicago, June 26, 1894

6.

EUGENE DEBS

The Carnegies and Rockefellers Tried to Silence Debs with Jail Time. That Didn't Stop Him

Socialist rabble-rouser Eugene Debs received almost a million votes for president more than once—even while he was in prison—as a member of the Socialist Party, which at one time was a powerful third party here in the United States. It captured the hearts and minds of millions of working-class people and intellectuals who supported a serious challenge to the status quo.

Debs ran for president the first time in 1900, in the era of the "robber barons," a brutal time economically for all but the very wealthy. The top 1 percent fought tooth and nail to keep every nickel they squeezed from the wage slaves whose twelve- and sixteen-hour days fueled the Industrial Revolution.

Eugene Debs helped organize the American Railway Union (ARU) in 1893 (see chapter 5), which shut down most rail travel west of Detroit when workers went on strike in the summer of 1894. Workers organized the strike after massive cuts in pay at the Pullman Palace Car Company and only returned to work after President Cleveland sent federal troops into Chicago to break up the strike. As an organizer of the strike, Debs received his first prison sentence.

In the six months he spent behind bars, Debs read a lot, including the works of Karl Marx. In 1901 he helped found the first Socialist Party in the United States, going on extended speaking tours and amassing a large following. Debs would run for president four times as the Socialist Party candidate, in 1904, 1908, 1912, and 1920.

It would be 2016 before a candidate with any socialist affiliation would get traction like that again—Bernie Sanders, the Democratic Socialist senator from Vermont.

The August 1912 issue of *La Follette's Weekly* (the precursor to the magazine *The Progressive*) ran several paragraphs of the acceptance speech Debs gave for the nomination by the Socialist Party. You can almost hear these words in the voice of Bernie Sanders:

> [The world's workers] have produced all of the world's wealth and supported all the world's governments. They have conquered all things but their own freedom. They are still the subject class in every nation on earth and the chief function of every government is to keep them at the mercy of their masters.
>
> There are no boundary lines to separate race from race, sex from sex, or creed from creed in the Socialist party. The common rights of all are equally recognized.
>
> . . . Every human being is entitled to sunlight and air, to what his labor produces, and to an equal chance with every other human being to unfold and ripen and give to the world the riches of his mind and soul.
>
> The Socialist Party is the one party which stands squarely and uncompromisingly for . . . one party pledged in every fiber of its being to the economic freedom of all the people.

Debs also helped found the Industrial Workers of the World (IWW). The "Wobblies," as they came to be known, were popular

Eugene V. Debs, 1897

Original American Railway Union pin. From the private collection of Davey MacBain

Debs delivering his antiwar speech in Canton, Ohio, for which he was arrested and charged with sedition

for some twenty years, becoming such a threat to the ruling class (and even to some of the more progressive wings of the Democratic and Republican parties) that, within a few years of the end of World War I, the IWW was effectively dismantled, although it still exists today. Many of its leaders were deported and jailed, and internal conflicts took a lot of its remaining energy.

In the lead-up to World War I, Debs and other members of the Socialist Party were increasingly watched and sometimes pursued under "sedition" laws. Debs offered this perspective on war in 1915:

> I am not a capitalist soldier; I am a proletarian revolutionist. I do not belong to the regular army of the plutocracy, but to the irregular army of the people. I refuse to obey any command to fight from the ruling class, but I will not wait to be commanded to

fight for the working class. I am opposed to every war but one; I am for that war with heart and soul, and that is the world-wide war of the social revolution. In that war I am prepared to fight in any way the ruling class may make it necessary, even to the barricades.

For its time, the 1912 Socialist Party platform was quite radical, including the following:

A minimum wage
An end to child labor
Rights for Black Americans
Improving working conditions
Increasing the number of people who can vote

The nerve of those Socialists! Just as Sanders forced the Democratic Party to the left in 2016, the popularity of Debs and the tenets of the Socialist Party pushed Democrats and even Republicans to be more progressive. In 1912, Debs won almost 6 percent of the popular vote.

As World War I raged, Eugene Debs delivered his final public speech in June 1918, at the Socialist Party convention. He spoke to a crowd of 1,200 near a jail where several of his fellow Socialist Party colleagues were housed for "antiwar agitation." He famously said:

It cannot be repeated too often—that the working class who fight all the battles, the working class who make the supreme sacrifices, the working class who freely shed their blood and furnish their corpses, have never yet had a voice in either declaring war or making peace. It is the ruling class that invariably does both. They alone declare war, and they alone make peace. Yours not to reason why; yours but to do and die.

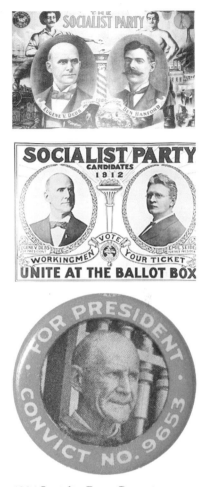

1904 Socialist Party Campaign Poster

1912 Socialist Party poster

1920 campaign button

That is their motto, and we object on the part of the awakening workers of this nation. If war is right let it be declared by the people. You who have your lives to lose, you certainly above all others have the right to decide the momentous issue of war or peace.

These words were used later to sentence Debs to prison for ten years under the Sedition Act of 1918. It was from his prison cell that he received nearly one million votes for president in 1920 (3.5 percent of the popular vote). He ran as simply "Convict No. 9653."

Debs's health deteriorated in the horrid prison conditions of the time, and president Warren G. Harding commuted his sentence in December 1921, when the war had ended and cooler heads prevailed in the country. Debs died in a sanitarium in 1926 from heart problems that developed during his time in prison.

There's a museum in his birthplace, Terre Haute, Indiana, that is well worth a visit; therein, you can see his handwritten quotes and the original publications they appeared in. Here are a few gems:

> *"I have no country to fight for; my country is the earth;*
> *I am a citizen of the world."*
> —"When I Shall Fight," *Appeal to Reason*, September 1915

> *"I am opposing a social order in which it is possible for one man*
> *who does absolutely nothing that is useful to amass a fortune of*
> *hundreds of millions of dollars, while millions of men and women*
> *who work all the days of their lives secure barely enough for a*
> *wretched existence."*
> —statement to the court upon being convicted of violating the Sedition Act, September 1918

"Those who produce should have, but we know that those who produce the most—that is, those who work hardest, and at the most difficult and most menial tasks, have the least."
–"Walls and Bars," 1927 (posthumous)

REFERENCES

Andrews, Evan. "7 Famous Presidential Pardons." History Stories, July 23, 2013. http://www.history.com/news/history-lists/7-famous-presidential-pardons.

Brendel, Martina. "The Pullman Strike." Illinois Periodicals Online. http://www.lib.niu.edu/1994/ihy941208.html.

Debs, Eugene V. "In What War Shall I Take Up Arms and Fight?" *Socialist Appeal* 3, no. 21 (April 4, 1939). Marxists Internet Archive. https://www.marxists.org/history/etol/newspape/themilitant/socialist-appeal-1939/v03n21/debs.htm.

Eugene V. Debs Foundation. "About the Museum." http://debsfoundation.org/index.php/landing/visit-the-museum/.

"History 1800's." History of Railroads & Rail Workers in the U.S. https://sites.google.com/site/historyofrrunions/home/early-history-1800-1899.

Industrial Workers of the World. "Fellow Worker Eugene V. Debs." IWW Biography. https://iww.org/history/biography/EugeneDebs/1.

Industrial Workers of the World. http://www.iww.org/.

Marxists Internet Archive. "Party History: Conventions of the Socialist Party of America." https://www.marxists.org/history/usa/eam/spa/socialistparty.html.

PBS. "The Sedition Act of 1918." Supreme Court History: Capitalism and Conflict. http://www.pbs.org/wnet/supremecourt/capitalism/sources_document1.html.

Sage American History. "The Socialist Party Platform of 1912." http://sageamericanhistory.net/progressive/docs/SocialistPlat1912.htm.

Stein, Jeff. "Bernie Sanders Moved Democrats to the Left. The Platform is Proof." *Vox*, July 25, 2016. http://www.vox.com/2016/7/25/12281022/the-democratic-party-platform.

Weber, Brandon. "Eugene Debs Got 1 Million Votes for President—As Convict Number 9653." *The Progressive*, November 2, 2016. http://progressive.org/dispatches/eugene-debs-got-1-million-votes-president-as-convict-number-9653/.

Zinn Education Project. "Eugene Debs: 'Canton, OH.'" Teaching *A People's History*. https://zinnedproject.org/materials/eugene-debs-canton-ohio/.

"I am opposing a social order in which it is possible for one man who does absolutely nothing that is useful to amass a fortune of hundreds of millions of dollars, while millions of men and women who work all the days of their lives secure barely enough for a wretched existence." —statement to the court upon being convicted of violating the Sedition Act, September 1918

7.

COLORADO'S MINING FRONTIER

Cripple Creek, 1894, and Ludlow, 1913:
Two Very Different Battles, and Both Were Shocking

PART I: CRIPPLE CREEK, 1894

One of the early strikes by miners in Colorado was marred by violence to a point that the union that represented them, the Western Federation of Miners (WFM), was later ostracized from mines in the region, though more often than not the violence was perpetrated by company-hired thugs. It was also the first time, and likely the last, that a state militia force was called out in support of a striking union rather than against it.

The hills in the region southwest of Pike's Peak were found to contain gold in 1891; less than ten years later, there were no less than five hundred mines operating there. Because there was a glut of mining labor after the silver mines took a serious hit during the stock market panic of 1893 (gold prices did not suffer a similar fate), three of the area's primary gold mine owners decided unilaterally in early 1894 that the miners who currently worked for them needed to work ten-hour days, but for the same pay of three dollars a day. Of course this didn't sit well with the people who did the work, so, after they formed the Western Federation of Miners (WFM) Local 19, the strike was on.

Within a month, area smelters were closing down, and several of the smaller mines gave in and accepted the original rate of three dollars for an eight-hour day. But the big boys held on.

Illegal sheriff's deputies under guard by the state militia, Cripple Creek, 1894

In early March, those mine owners decided they wanted to reopen. They sought and obtained injunctions to prevent strikers from interfering with production or replacement workers, and then they hired strikebreakers—scabs, as most union people have referred to them for centuries. On March 16, a group of armed strikers ambushed six deputies sent by county sheriff M. F. Bowers, charged with enforcing the injunctions, who were on their way to the mining town of Victor to do just that. When they hit the town of Altman, they were attacked, and one of them was shot through the arm. When the dust settled, the Altman judge, who was a member of the WFM, found the deputies guilty of carrying concealed weapons and disturbing the peace, and sent them back to Cripple Creek, weaponless.

The net effect of altercations such as this was that potential scabs didn't feel at all safe in taking work from the striking miners. It was also clear that, since the WFM had done its job well of getting its own people elected to various positions in most of the town governments around the mining communities, it would be hard for the mine bosses to pull those strings. Last, Colorado governor Davis H. Waite had recently been elected as a member of the Populist Party, and he was very sympathetic to the miners as well.

Sheriff Bowers sounded the alarm with that very same governor the next day, and three hundred state militia troops were sent to Cripple Creek to help maintain law and order. Meanwhile, Bowers ordered the arrest of several of the Altman officials as well as the union president. They met with the general in charge of militia troops, who found that none of the miners had resisted arrest and, in fact, went willingly—and then were promptly bailed out.

The general declared that he would not assist the deputies with any of their duties, because he was there to preserve the peace and protect both sides. The mine owners then closed the mines, rather than try to stay open.

In early May, the companies came back to the table with the offer of $2.75 a day for eight hours. The WFM refused, and things stayed pretty much the same. Shortly thereafter, however, owners of the involved mine companies met privately with Sheriff Bowers and offered him the money and sufficient weapons to deputize a small army of one hundred. He agreed. The miners got wind of this and sent union president John Calderwood out to collect funds so that their strike could continue. He asked former army officer Junius J. Johnson to fill in while he was gone. This was rather prescient; Johnson put his military skills to use immediately as he established a camp on top of Bull Hill, a steep bluff that overlooked the town of Altman. He also began training the miners in military-style maneuvers and enlisted their help in getting the commissary fully stocked. In other words, he was preparing for siege warfare.

A few days later, 125 deputies arrived and began to set up camp within view of Bull Hill. The miners sent some men down to "greet" them, which meant that the deputies began to head quickly in the other direction. Those same miners left some dynamite charges in the Strong mine shaft house nearby and promptly detonated same. The steam house was also quickly dynamited, raining iron, dirt, cable, and timber onto the deputies. They were not going to have any more of this and promptly began the process of leaving town entirely.

There was one more altercation: some of the miners decided to steal a work train and head toward the fleeing deputies; they caught up with them and a battle ensued that left one dead on each side, along with several prisoners, who were exchanged quickly. In this way as well as many others, this was almost like an actual war.

In late May, the mining companies met again with Sheriff Bowers; this time, they wanted

1,200 deputies—and they were willing to pay for every last one of them.

It all came to a head on May 27 and 28, when Governor Waite again got involved. He ordered the miners off of Bull Hill, while at the same time designating the 1,200 deputies as an illegal force. He also let the state militia know they were needed—and soon. As the state forces arrived and began to congregate in the Cripple Creek area, the deputies took advantage of the situation and began firing on the miners atop Bull Hill and harassing citizens of Cripple Creek. The chaos was finally interrupted by the militia, which eventually disarmed the deputies and ushered them through town while the miners willingly left Bull Hill to the friendly visitors sent by Governor Waite.

The Western Federation of Miners agreed to go back to eight hours a day for the full three dollars a day (which became the standard, going forward, for mine worker agreements in the West), and in return, they also agreed to allow nonunion miners who might be sent to work in their midst to do their jobs in peace. Of course, those of us who have worked in a strong union environment know how that goes—eventually, the nonunion people are won over.

The WFM flourished in the months to follow, organizing hotels, restaurants, laundry workers, newsboys, and more. It eventually had two hundred local unions in thirteen Western states. It also enjoyed political support throughout the region as it grew and thrived. As many of the traditional labor unions across the United States became politically more conservative, the WFM actually helped to create the Industrial Workers of the World (IWW) (see chapter 6) and remained fairly radical throughout its existence.

There were several other important union drives and strikes in Colorado over the next few decades—the Ludlow strike and

Cripple Creek under martial law, 1894

Reproduction of original union pin, Western Federation of Miners. From the private collection of Davey MacBain

massacre being one of the major events—but Cripple Creek was really the beginning of these miners' deciding to take some of their fate into their own hands, to wrest from the mine owners a little more control of their working conditions and a bit more of a piece of the golden pie that they dug, shoveled, and pick-axed every day of their working lives.

REFERENCES

"Cripple Creek, Colorado." Western Mining History. https://www.westernmininghistory.com/towns/colorado/cripple-creek.

Glenn, Joshua and Mark Kingwell. *The Wage Slave's Glossary.* Windsor, Ontario: Biblioasis, 2011.

Rasmussen, Ryan, "Colorado's Role in the American Labor Struggle: Western Unionism and the Labor Question 1894–1914." Undergraduate Honors Thesis, University of Colorado, Boulder, 2013. http://scholar.colorado.edu/cgi/viewcontent.cgi?article=1750&context=honr_theses.

Rastall, Benjamin. *The Labor History of the Cripple Creek District, A Study in Industrial Evolution.* Charleston, SC: Nabu Press, 2014.

PART II: LUDLOW, 1913

THE LUDLOW MASSACRE

The early 1900s were a time of great social upheaval in our country. During the years leading up to the Ludlow Massacre, miners all around the country, looking to make a better life for themselves and their families, set up picket lines, organized massive parades and rallies, and even took up arms.

Some died.

COAL COUNTRY, COLORADO

A hundred years ago, the Rocky Mountains were the source of a vast supply of coal. At its peak, the coal industry employed sixteen thousand people and accounted for 10 percent of all employed workers in the state of Colorado. Most of the miners were immigrants—many of them Greek—and it was dangerous work; in just 1913 alone, the mines claimed the lives of more than a hundred people. There were laws in place that were supposed to protect workers, but management largely ignored them, which led to Colorado having an on-the-job fatality rate fully double that of any other mining state.

Ludlow tent colony before the massacre, April 20, 1914. Image via University of Denver

It was the era of company towns, when all of a town's real estate, housing, doctors' practices, and grocery stores were owned by the coal companies. This arrangement led to the suppression of dissent as well as inflated prices and an extreme dependence on the coal companies for everything that made life livable. In some of these places, workers couldn't even leave town—and armed guards made sure they didn't. Also, if any miner or his family began to air grievances, they might find themselves evicted, with their belongings out on the street and themselves run out of town.

THE UNION

The United Mine Workers of America (UMWA) had been organizing for many years in the area. Colorado Fuel and Iron, one of the biggest companies in the West, was owned by the Rockefeller family, notoriously anti-union. Put all this together, and it was a powder keg.

STRIKE!

When a strike was called in 1913, the coal company evicted all the miners from their company homes, and they moved to tent villages on leased land set up by the UMWA. Company-hired guards (known as "goons") and members of the Colorado National Guard would drive by the tent villages and randomly shoot into the tents, leading the strikers to dig holes beneath the tents and the wooden beams that supported them, to dive into when guns were fired.

Why did the union call for a strike? The workers wanted the following:

- Recognition of the union as bargaining agent

- An increase in tonnage rates (equivalent to a 10 percent wage increase)

- Enforcement of the eight-hour workday

The "Death Special" improvised armored car. Image via University of Denver

The "Death Pit," where eleven children and two women died after their tent was set on fire by mine militia and the military. Image via University of Denver

- Payment for "dead work" that usually wasn't compensated, such as laying coal car tracks

- The job known as "weight-checkmen" to be a position elected by workers. This was to keep company weight-checkmen honest, so the workers got paid for their true work

- The right to use any store rather than just the company store, and to choose their own houses and doctors

- Strict enforcement of Colorado's laws, especially mine safety laws

THE POWDER KEG EXPLODES

The attacks from the goons continued, as did the battles between scabs (strikebreakers) and the miners, culminating in an attack on April 20, 1914. Company goons and Colorado National Guard soldiers kidnapped and later killed the main camp leader and some of his fellow miners, and then set the tents in the main camp ablaze with kerosene. As they were engulfed in flames, people inside the tents tried to flee the inferno; many were shot as they tried to escape. Some also died in the dugouts below the burning tents. Two women and eleven children died in the fire directly above them. A day that started off with Orthodox Easter celebrations for many of the families became known as the Ludlow Massacre.

Cavalry, led by General Chase, attack a group of women protesting the arrest and imprisonment of Mary Harris "Mother" Jones. Image via University of Denver

THE TEN-DAY WAR

The miners, whose friends and family members had just been murdered, beseeched president Woodrow Wilson to put a stop to the madness, but he deferred to the governor, who was in the pocket of the mine companies. News of the murders spread, and protests were held in many cities around the country, some following Rockefeller as he moved in social circles. Protests were even held at his church in New York City.

The miners did what they had to do. Ludlow strikers quickly armed themselves, knowing that many other confrontations were coming soon. Then they went to the mines being operated by scabs and forced many of them to close, sometimes setting fire to the buildings. The battle raged along a forty-mile front at several mines.

Mother Jones was a prominent union activist and eventual cofounder of the Industrial Workers of the World (IWW), who came to Colorado to help the strikers, especially by organizing the wives and children of the strikers—a specialty of hers.

After ten solid days of pitched battle and sixty-six men, women, and children killed on both sides, the president finally sent in the National Guard, which promptly disarmed both sides.

UNION VICTORY

While more than one hundred people died over the course of about eighteen months before and after the battles at Ludlow, and the union ultimately lost the election, the Ludlow Massacre spurred a congressional investigation that led to the beginnings of child-labor laws and an eight-hour workday in the United States, among other things.

It also brought national attention to the plight of these miners and their families, and it showed the resilience and strength that union people could display when they remained united, even in the face of extreme corporate and government violence. Historian Howard Zinn called it "the culminating act of perhaps the most violent struggle between corporate power and laboring men in American history." And the primary mine owner, John D. Rockefeller Jr., received a lot of the criticism and blame for what had happened.

The UMWA is still a solid union today, and there is a monument in Colorado to those who died in the Ludlow Massacre.

REFERENCES

Auerbach, Jonathan. *Weapons of Democracy: Propaganda, Progressivism, and American Public Opinion*. Baltimore: Johns Hopkins University Press, 2015.

Colorado Coal Field War Project. "A History of the Colorado Coal Field War." https://www.du.edu/ludlow/cfhist3.html.

History.com. "Militia Slaughters Strikers at Ludlow." This Day in History, 2009. http://www.history.com/this-day-in-history/militia-slaughters-strikers-at-ludlow-colorado.

Loomis, Eric. "US Workers Were Once Massacred Fighting for the Protections Being Rolled Back Today." Moyers & Company, April 23, 2014. http://billmoyers.com/2014/04/23/us-workers-were-once-massacred-fighting-for-the-protections-being-rolled-back-today/.

Ludlow: Greek Americans in the Colorado Mine War. Directed by Leonidas Vardaros. Kallithea, Greece: Apostolis Berdebes, 2016.

SparkNotes Editors. "SparkNote on Mother Jones." SparkNotes LLC. 2005. http://www.sparknotes.com/biography/motherjones/.

Trembath, Brian K. "Remembering Colorado's Coal Wars . . . And Coal Miners." Denver Public Library, September 2, 2015. https://history.denverlibrary.org/news/remembering-colorados-coal-wars.

Zinn Education Project. "Ludlow Massacre: April 20, 1914." Teaching *A People's History*. https://zinnedproject.org/materials/ludlow-massacre.

A Ludlow striker and family. Image via University of Denver

8.

TRIANGLE SHIRTWAIST FIRE

One Hundred Twenty-Three Young Women Who Went to Work One Day in a New York Factory Never Came Home. It Changed Our Country Forever

There has been a lot written about the Triangle Shirtwaist Factory Fire in Manhattan, 1911. This disaster was one of the most significant events leading to changes in workplace safety regulations and practices, at least for the United States.

When the workforce—almost entirely young women—went to their jobs the morning of March 25, 1911, they had no idea that their lives, and eventually those of millions of workers across the United States, would be forever altered that day.

Some lives ended when they hurled themselves to the sidewalk from many stories up. Some were consumed in the inferno. Some people were injured or physically scarred for life—and most were mentally scarred.

The Triangle Shirtwaist factory, located in Manhattan, employed several hundred mostly immigrant women and girls. It was a true sweatshop; work was long and arduous—sometimes eighty or more hours a week, for fifteen dollars per week.

The conditions were appalling. There were four elevators, but only one worked, and it was at the

end of a long, narrow corridor. There were two stairwells, but one was kept locked, ostensibly to keep workers from stealing. The other stairwell was at the end of a long corridor and had a door that opened inward, rather than outward. There were no sprinkler systems, and while there was a fire escape, it was woefully inadequate to support hundreds of people if the worst happened.

The worst did, indeed, happen.

On Saturday, March 25, a rag bin caught fire. An attempt to put that out was fruitless, as the fire hose was old and broken,

Mourners, ten days after the Triangle Shirtwaist fire

and the valve was rusted shut. As people began to panic, every system that should have worked, had it been in decent condition, failed: the elevator was used to cart a few dozen workers down, and it broke soon in the heat. The first casualties happened when the women waiting to use the now failed elevator plunged down its shaft to their death—or they would have been burned alive.

The girls who fled via the stairwells were trapped at the locked doors and trampled, and all were eventually consumed by fire. A few people, including the owners, escaped by heading for the roof and then jumping to surrounding buildings.

As firefighters arrived, they witnessed the absolute horror of young women hurling themselves out of the windows to their deaths on the streets and sidewalks below. Some of the rescuers were puzzled to see bundles of garments and clothing on the sidewalk below the building, only to recoil in shock when they realized they were the bodies of women who had plunged to their deaths rather than be burned alive.

It took less than twenty minutes for all of this to transpire, and a total of 145 died from the Triangle Shirtwaist Fire.

After such a tragedy, it would be understandable for most survivors to mourn and then go on with life as it was—or simply give up. Not for the survivors of Triangle Shirtwaist. Though it was a non-union shop, some of these women and girls were members of the International Ladies Garment Workers Union (ILGWU). The survivors, joined by women from other shops around the city that were in similarly horrid shape and at risk of the same kind of tragedy, got together and demanded change.

On April 5, just ten days later, eighty thousand people showed up on New York's Fifth Avenue, one of the most prominent streets of the city. They marched, and they proclaimed that this would not happen again, they organized, and they mourned. The ILGWU proposed an official day of mourning to soon follow the march on Fifth Avenue; 350,000 showed up for the funeral march.

The union organized relief efforts for the survivors, who included orphaned children, and they helped the women who were injured to recuperate and to be able to survive financially while doing so. It was a large humanitarian effort, given the scope of the tragedy, and organizations like the American Red Cross got involved as well.

JUSTICE? NOT FOR THE 1 PERCENT

Eventually, a grand jury indicted the owners, Mr. Harris and Mr. Blanck, on manslaughter charges, but a jury could not find them guilty. Various civil suits were brought, and they settled on paying seventy-five dollars per life. However, the owners' insurance policy paid them four hundred dollars per life—for a net gain to them of sixty thousand dollars. Harris and Blanck were cited multiple times in the years following, after they opened new factories, for locked doors, inadequate fire escapes, and other violations.

But the real effects of the fire and deaths were legislation that mandated fire safety and other workplace safety regulations in every shop in the state of New York. This included enforcement of those regulations via a new State Department of Labor, and working conditions improved substantially. This, then, became a model for the rest of the nation to follow. In fact, some of the rights guaranteed by the National Labor Relations Act in 1935 were a direct result of the fallout from the fire, including the rights of workers to collectively address safety issues on the job, and even to walk out if those safety issues were not resolved. Many of these ideas were championed by some of the very people who witnessed the Triangle fire and changed employment laws in the state of New York to favor workers.

The Triangle tragedy also spurred union organizing drives, and according to Bruce Raynor, president of Workers United (which is what the ILGWU eventually morphed into), "It created a strong garment workers union. It helped to really start the modern labor movement."

One of the first photos taken of the fire

Bodies of workers who jumped to escape the fire

REFERENCES

AFL-CIO. "Triangle Shirtwaist Fire." Key Events in Labor History. https://www.aflcio.org/About/Our-History/Key-Events-in-Labor-History/Triangle-Shirtwaist-Fire.

Cornell University. "Investigation and Trial." The 1911 Triangle Factory Fire. http://trianglefire.ilr.cornell.edu/story/investigationTrial.html.

Cornell University. "Legislative Reform at State and Local Level." The 1911 Triangle Factory Fire. http://trianglefire.ilr.cornell.edu/legacy

/legislativereform.html.

History.com. "Triangle Shirtwaist Factory Fire." 2009. http://www.history
.com/topics/triangle-shirtwaist-fire.

Matthews, Karen. "1911 Triangle Fire Remembered as Spur to Unions, Safety Laws." *USA Today*, March 22, 2011. http://usatoday30.usatoday
.com/money/workplace/2011-03-22-triangle-fire-remembered.htm.

PBS, "The American Experience: Triangle Fire." http://www.pbs.org/wgbh
/americanexperience/films/triangle/#part01.

United States Department of Labor. "Aftermath." The Triangle Shirtwaist
Factory Fire of 1911. https://www.dol.gov/shirtwaist/aftermath.htm.

9.

CHRISTMAS EVE, 1913

Fifty-Nine Children Died on Christmas Eve, 1913, and It Broke Hearts Around the World

I n July 1913, more than seven thousand miners and members of the Western Federation of Miners (WFM) struck the C&H Copper Mining Company in Calumet, Michigan. It was largely the usual issues of people who worked for a big company during a time when capitalists ran roughshod over workers—in other words, a time when monopolies were a way of life.

Strikers' demands included pay raises, an end to child labor, and safer conditions, including an end to one-man drill operations, which could lead to mine collapses and other safety problems, and a demand for support beams in the mines (which mine owners didn't want because support beams were costly, but miners killed in cave-ins "do not cost us anything.")

Six months without work left many of the miners' families with little food for the holidays and no money for gifts, so the Ladies' Auxiliary of the Western Federation of Miners held a Christmas party for the kids. On Christmas Eve, 1913, five hundred children and two hundred adults came to the party, held on the second floor of Calumet's Italian Hall. The only way in and out was a very steep stairway that led to the only door.

As darkness fell and people began to go home to their family celebrations, some of the children gathered around the stage as presents were passed out—for many, it would be the only gift they'd receive this year, and they knew it. In the middle of this festive celebration, someone—possibly more than one person—opened the door at the bottom of the staircase and yelled, "FIRE!"

Absolute chaos ensued. As everybody ran down the stairs to the exit, some tripped, and then others fell on top of them. Some at the time claimed the door was blocked from the outside, though this has been disputed ever since. Regardless, children and adults were trampled, then suffocated, by the throng of bodies trying to escape the "fire"—which didn't actually exist.

In all, seventy-three people, including fifty-nine children, died, most of them Finnish immigrants. The youngest was Rafael Lesar, two and a half years old. The oldest was Kate Pitteri, sixty-six years old.

Some families lost all of their children, like Frank and Josepa Klarich, who buried their three daughters, Kristina, eleven; Maria, nine; and Katarina, seven. Their little crosses are lined up in a row over their graves in a cemetery west of Calumet still today.

The culprit or culprits who yelled into the hall that day to cause the tragedy were never identified, but it's widely suspected that it was allies of mine management or the owners, who did so to disrupt the miners' party. It was never clear whether they knew what would happen by causing the stampede of human beings, and nobody was ever prosecuted or even arrested for causing the massacre. It is always thus: those with money and power control the narrative, silence the truth, and thwart justice.

Italian Hall was demolished in the 1980s, but especially during the holiday season, the people of Calumet still talk of that night, more than one hundred years ago, when so many innocents perished.

Partly because a lot of miners left the town of Calumet after this tragedy, the strike didn't accomplish what the miners wanted. However, it's considered a turning point for union strength

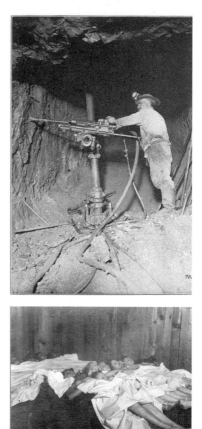

A one-man drill operation

Some of the children who died in the tragedy

in Michigan's Copper Country. One can imagine that "remember Calumet" was the rallying cry on the minds and in the hearts of unions all around the area for decades afterward.

In 1941, Woody Guthrie got an idea for a song about the tragedy, which he called "1913 Massacre." Ella Reeve "Mother" Bloor's eyewitness account in her 1940 book, *We Are Many*, inspired him to write the piece. Mother Bloor was a labor organizer who was active in the Western Federation of Miners, the union that represented the people who were on strike in Calumet.

Italian Hall, Calumet, Michigan. Image via Michigan Tech Archives

"1913 MASSACRE"

Words and music by Woody Guthrie

Take a trip with me in 1913,
To Calumet, Michigan, in the copper country.
I will take you to a place called Italian Hall,
Where the miners are having their big
　　Christmas ball.

I will take you in a door and up a high stairs,
Singing and dancing is heard everywhere,
I will let you shake hands with the people you see,
And watch the kids dance around the big
　　Christmas tree.

You ask about work and you ask about pay,
They'll tell you they make less than a dollar a day,
Working the copper claims, risking their lives,
So it's fun to spend Christmas with children and wives.

There's talking and laughing and songs in the air,
And the spirit of Christmas is there everywhere,
Before you know it you're friends with us all,
And you're dancing around and around in the hall.

Well a little girl sits down by the Christmas tree lights,
To play the piano so you gotta keep quiet,

To hear all this fun you would not realize,
That the copper boss's thug men are milling outside.

The copper boss's thugs stuck their heads in the door,
One of them yelled and he screamed, "there's a fire,"
A lady she hollered, "there's no such a thing.
Keep on with your party, there's no such thing."

A few people rushed and it was only a few,
"It's just the thugs and the scabs fooling you,"
A man grabbed his daughter and carried her down,
But the thugs held the door and he could not get out.

And then others followed, a hundred or more,
But most everybody remained on the floor,
The gun thugs they laughed at their murderous joke,
While the children were smothered on the stairs by the door.

Such a terrible sight I never did see,
We carried our children back up to their tree,
The scabs outside still laughed at their spree,
And the children that died there were seventy-three.

The piano played a slow funeral tune,
And the town was lit up by a cold Christmas moon,
The parents they cried and the miners they moaned,
"See what your greed for money has done."

REFERENCES

Baker, Frederick Jr. Review of *Death's Door: The Truth Behind Michigan's Largest Mass Murder* by Steve Lehto. *Michigan Bar Journal*, September 2007. http://www.superiorreading.com/pdf/lehto.bakerreview.1.pdf.

Genealogica. "The Italian Hall Disaster, Calumet, Michigan." http://www.genealogia.fi/emi/emi3d31e.htm.

Lehto, Steve. *Italian Hall: The Official Transcript of the Coroner's Inquest.* Troy, MI: Momentum Books, 2007.

Lehto, Steve. "The Italian Hall Disaster: One Reason to Observe a Silent Night This Christmas Eve." *Huffington Post*, January 23, 2014. http://www.huffingtonpost.com/steve-lehto/the-italian-hall-disaster _b_1120771.html.

Penn, Allie. "No News Is Good News: Newspaper Reports of Calumet's Italian Hall Disaster." *Upper Country: A Journal of the Lake Superior Region* 4, no 4 (2007). https://commons.nmu.edu/upper_country/vol4 /iss1/4.

Thelen, Greg. "Copper Strike 1913–14." Michigan Technological University. October 11, 2015. http://ss.sites.mtu.edu/mhugl/2015/10/11 /the-houghton-county-copper-strike-of-1913-14/.

10.

CHRISTMAS TRUCE

These Soldiers Were Thought to Be Enemies, but They Played Soccer and Celebrated Christmas Eve, 1914, Together

Trench warfare in World War I was absolutely brutal. The Western Front of the war in 1914 included trenches where French and English soldiers awaited the next attack from the Germans (or vice versa), or simply wallowed in the frost and mud, biding their time. They were within less than the length of a football field in some places—as close as sixty to eighty yards—from the enemy.

So close that the soldiers could sometimes hear each other talk, or cough. Or even sing.

The region between the men, past the barbed wire, was known as "no man's land," and it's where, one Christmas Eve, some of them met as humans rather than as enemies.

Early on in the war, there was some fraternization between the enemy lines, with soldiers from England and France making contact with their enemies from Germany. They exchanged cigarettes, chocolate, and whisky, learning some words of each other's languages—maybe even some curse words—and tossing verbal jabs back and forth. Eventually, some soldiers agreed to leave one another alone and get out of the disease- and death-ridden trenches to exercise or just enjoy breakfast in the morning rather than shoot at each other.

There were widespread calls for peace that holiday season, with even Pope Benedict XV asking

for a Christmas truce on December 7, 1914, with these words:
" . . . that the guns may fall silent at least upon the night the
angels sang." Though Germany agreed to this, the leadership of
other countries refused.

On Christmas Eve that year, some parts of the front lines
began a temporary truce to collect and bury the dead. Soon, it became an exchange between French and German troops of newspapers, cigarettes, words, and song. Many of the German soldiers
put up tiny Christmas trees on the edges of their trenches. These
were gifts from home, and they lit candles in their branches.

Carols began to ring out—"O Tannenbaum" from the German side, which of course was "O, Christmas Tree" for the English. "Adeste Fidelis" ("O Come, All Ye Faithful") followed on
both sides, too.

Forever after referred to as the "Christmas Truce," it spread
to many sections of the Western Front that night, and came to
symbolize the feelings shared by many soldiers that this war was
not something they'd chosen to fight in, and that these men were
not people they wanted to shoot at—and perhaps they'd rather

be celebrating with them.

As they got to know each other, you can imagine the soldiers wondering who was in their sights when they pulled the trigger. It probably even stopped some of them from doing just that. Was the human being in their sights across the way someone they had just shared a chocolate bar with the previous day, while learning a few words of his language? Or hearing, in broken English/French/German, about their family back home? It rather humanized the soldiers to each other.

In some places up and down the lines, the truce lasted until New Year's Day. Eventually, the high command on both sides, hearing of the troops that had met on Christmas Eve of 1914, issued orders for such things to cease. Because—of course.

And sadly, just a few years later, the war had become so brutal and the casualties so massive that this kind of fraternization no longer happened. It was as if a silent shroud had descended between the men that turned them into something other than what they were that night—fellow human beings, very much alike.

Immortalized in the John McCutcheon song "Christmas in the Trenches," the event has inspired many to rethink why we do what we do to each other as human beings when we fight in wars. Featuring the fictional Francis Tolliver but based on the true story of the Christmas Truce, the closing lyrics of the song sum it up perfectly:

> *My name is Francis Tolliver, in Liverpool I dwell,*
> *Each Christmas come since World War I I've learned its lessons well,*
> *That the ones who call the shots won't be among the dead and lame,*
> *And on each end of the rifle we're the same.*

(Author's note: While almost everything in this book is about American workers and soldiers, this particular part of history took place before the United States entered WWI in 1917. Including this chapter is intentional, because it shows the ability of soldiers to see beyond their weapons and realize what it is they are impelled to do to each other. McCutcheon's lyrics say it best: "The ones who call the shots won't be among the dead and lame / And on each end of the rifle we're the same."

That is the spirit in which this story is offered. Also, I like to think that, if it were US soldiers that Christmas Eve, they'd have been right there with the Allies, offering their cigarettes and candy and trading stories with the "enemy.")

REFERENCES

Hagerty, Edward. "The Night the Angels Sang: Christmas 1914 at Home and on the Front." *Saber and Scroll* 4, no. 1 (2015). http://digitalcommons.apus.edu /saberandscroll/vol4/iss1/3/.

History.com. "Life in a Trench." World War I History. http://www.history.com/topics /world-war-i/world-war-i-history/videos/life-in-a-trench.

National Library of Scotland. "British First World War Trench Maps: 1915–1918." http://maps.nls.uk/ww1/trenches/info1.html.

Weihnachtsfriede (Christmas Peace)

British and German officers meeting in "no man's land," Christmas, 1914

11.

THE BATTLE OF BLAIR MOUNTAIN

It Ended When Federal Troops Were Called Against Thirteen Thousand Miners. It Was "Civil War in the Hills"

What happens when you decide to mess with a bunch of hardscrabble miners and take away their jobs, their wages, their food, and their houses? Well, what actually happened was the West Virginia Mine Wars, as they're still referred to today.

Like many stories included here, the West Virginia Mine Wars are critical to understanding the history of the labor movement in the United States. The Battle of Blair Mountain, for example, was—and still is—the most violent labor confrontation in history, in which union-supportive coal miners fought against local government and a coal company–funded militia, eventually involving the US Army.

"COAL COUNTRY," WEST VIRGINIA

In the late 1800s in West Virginia, it wasn't easy to be a coal miner. For starters, mining wasn't just a job, it was a way of life—and a hard way of life, at that. You lived in a company town, bought all your food and supplies at the company store, were paid in company money called "scrip," sent your kids to the company school, read the company paper, obeyed the company-employed police . . . on and on.

Because the coal companies controlled every aspect of the miners' lives, the companies could do whatever they wanted: pay as little as they felt like; teach what they felt like; wrap the miners in a cycle of bare-bones survival as they saw fit; and even turn out whole families into the rainy night, if the miner who lived with them dared challenge the status quo or utter the word "union" within earshot of anybody who wanted to be a stooge for Big Coal.

Coal cars near the company store, McDowell County, West Virginia

The job was rife with danger. Fatal accidents were frequent, and illnesses such as black lung disease claimed miners and their families alike. As the decades wore on, the owners of these coal companies kept raking in the profits. The fledgling United Mine Workers of America (UMWA) began to gain a foothold in many parts of the country, including West Virginia, and the union fought for a better way of life for these people.

But southern West Virginia stayed mostly nonunion, and the coal companies were quite determined to keep it that way. The stakes were high, as was the tension between workers and their bosses. It eventually exploded into what is to this day the largest armed insurrection since the Civil War.

INCEPTION: PAINT CREEK

The Paint Creek-Cabin Creek strike of 1912, near Charleston, West Virginia, was the first major demonstration of the violence to come as miners and their families stood up for their rights. Coal miners were fed up with the low wages and the poor working conditions—loading tons of coal for weeks, months, and years on end in the cramped, dark mines, only to find themselves deeper in debt at the end of each day, living in company towns.

The miners demanded the right to unionize, the right to free speech and assembly, the right to be paid accurately and in

West Virginia coal mine

real US dollars rather than the company scrip, and more. They were tired of being cheated out of their already meager wages. You see, being paid by the ton and having no access to scales, they had no choice but to take their earnings at the word of the company weigh men. "Sixteen tons? Nah, that's only twelve today. You got a problem with that?"

When nearly ten thousand miners finally went on strike, their protests were largely nonviolent. Until, that is, the mine operators called in the notorious Baldwin-Felts Detective Agency to break up the strike. More than three hundred armed men descended on the area on behalf of Baldwin-Felts. Beatings were common, and sniper attacks and sabotage were also used. Union-sympathetic miners and their families were often forcefully taken from their homes and tossed into the hills to live in tents and tent colonies, and inside these tents, people were starving.

THE "BULL MOOSE SPECIAL"

The tent colonies were soon subject to a new tactic from the company goons—a heavily armored train that the miners called the "Bull Moose Special" was sent through one of the tent colonies, firing machine guns and high-powered rifles at tents, even killing some of the miners.

In a Senate committee investigation that followed, as reported by the Wichita *Times*, one woman described her encounter with the train:

> Mrs. Annie Hill, who limped into the committee room, told how she shielded her three little children from the bullets by hiding them in the chimney corner of her little home at Holly Grove when the armored train made its appearance. She said she had been shot through the limbs and the bullet had gone through the Bible and hymnbook on her parlor table.

Martial law was declared. Mary Harris "Mother" Jones (a feisty union activist in her seventies, who had come to the area to help the miners) was arrested and imprisoned.

After nearly twelve months, at least fifty people lay dead. The number grew when counting those who had succumbed to starvation and sickness from the near siege-like conditions in

Typical coal miner dwellings, McDowell County, West Virginia

the tents and on the streets. The battles went back and forth, with miners gathering to support their brethren during a few pitched battles, which were followed by declarations of martial law. A new governor, Henry D. Hatfield, finally sought peace with terms favorable to the miners, and things quieted down.

A MASSACRE IN MATEWAN

Six years later, unionized miners in other parts of the country were seeing huge victories—such as a 27 percent pay increase and the right to unionize. This inspired the miners around Matewan, West Virginia, to join the United Mine Workers of America in record numbers. By the spring of 1920, three thousand Matewan miners had joined.

The Stone Mountain Coal Company quickly retaliated. This time, the miners had key public officials on their side: both the mayor and Sheriff Sid Hatfield. So when the coal company called in the Baldwin-Felts men (or the "Baldwin Thugs," as the miners knew them), Sheriff Hatfield met them at the train station. After a brief verbal tussle, the Baldwin Thugs carried on, throwing six mining families and all of their possessions out of their homes and into the rain.

Word spread fast, and soon an enraged group of miners headed to the train station where Sheriff Hatfield had promised to arrest the Baldwin men. The two forces came together on the steps of the Chambers Hardware Store. When the dust had settled, the mayor was shot, seven Baldwin-Felts detectives were killed, and two miners were dead.

Sheriff Hatfield—who claimed credit for the deaths of two Baldwin Thugs—became a hero. This was the first time the seemingly invincible Baldwin Thugs had been defeated, giving the miners hope.

In the spring of 1921, charges against Hatfield and his men were either dismissed or they were found not guilty. The enraged Baldwin-Felts crew swore vengeance, and just a few months later, they killed Sheriff Hatfield and his deputy on the steps of the county courthouse.

Nearly two thousand people marched in their funeral procession. It wound its way through the town of Matewan and to the cemetery in neighboring Kentucky. As the rage built among the miners, it headed toward a final confrontation—the Battle of Blair Mountain.

THE BATTLE OF BLAIR MOUNTAIN

The culmination of decades of mistreatment by the mining companies and years of rising tensions came to a head with the Battle of Blair Mountain. It was just after the Matewan Massacre, and thousands of miners began pouring out of the mountains to take up arms against the villains who had attacked their families, assassinated their hero, and mistreated them for decades. The miners wore red bandanas around their necks to distinguish themselves from the company men, who wore white patches, and to avoid getting shot by their own troops. (This is actually where the term "rednecks" comes from.)

The sheriff of Little Coal River sent in law enforcement to keep the miners at bay, but the miners captured the troopers, disarmed them, and sent them running. The West Virginia governor also lost his chance for a peaceful resolution when, after meeting with some of the miners' leaders, he chose to reject their demands.

The miners were thirteen thousand strong as they headed toward the nonunion territory of Logan and Mingo counties. They faced Sheriff Chafin—who was financially supported by the coal companies—and his two thousand men, who acted as security, police, and militia. Chafin stationed many of his troops in the hills around Blair Mountain, West Virginia. From there, Chafin dropped tear gas and pipe bombs on the miners.

For a moment, it seemed like the confrontation might come to an end when a ceasefire agreement was made, and many of the miners began to head home. But the ceasefire broke when Sheriff Chafin's men were found shooting miners and their families in the streets of Sharples, West Virginia, just beyond Blair Mountain.

UMWA logo

UMWA officials and members of the "miners' army" display the bomb dropped on them during the Battle of Blair Mountain

THE FEDS ARE CALLED UP

On August 30, 1921, president Warren Harding intervened, placing all of West Virginia under martial law. Harding sent fourteen planes to West Virginia that were fully armed for combat but were only used for surveillance. According to Robert Shogan, "the Federal force that mattered most were the infantry units that began arriving ... [on] September 2, some 2,100 strong."

The miners never made it through Chafin's lines—and it's hard to say what would've happened if they had, but likely it would have meant all-out war between the troops and the miners. After one million rounds were fired, the miners retreated. It was time to go home and fight another day.

More than a hundred people had been killed—about thirty on Chafin's side and fifty to one hundred on the union miners' side. Almost one thousand of the miners were indicted for murder and treason, and many more lost their jobs.

In the short term, the defeat of the striking miners was devastating to the UMWA. Membership plummeted from fifty thousand to ten thousand over the next several years. It took until 1935—post–Great Depression and FDR's New Deal—for the rest of the mines in southern West Virginia to become unionized.

However, a single battle doesn't tell the whole story of the larger fight for justice. In the end, the coal companies lost more than they gained. These bloody conflicts drew the nation's attention to the plight of the long-suffering mine workers, and unions began to understand that they needed to fight for laws that allowed them to organize and that penalized companies that broke the law every chance they got.

These moral victories allowed a number of other unions, like the United Auto Workers and the United Steelworkers of America after them, to flourish as well. Each battle laid some groundwork for the next. Each of these fights in West Virginia solidified the resolve and desire of the miners and their families to stand up for their rights to improve their lot in life.

For these brave workers, the American dream was something they had to fight for, something they sometimes died for, and something they wanted to pass on to future generations, despite the efforts of the coal companies to prevent them.

Nearly a hundred years after workers laid down their lives for the right to fair employment, their story has taken root inside the building that used to be the Chambers Hardware Store in downtown Matewan: the first museum to tell the story of these brave people opened in 2015.

"[Matewan was] a symbolic moment in a larger, broader and continuing historical struggle-in the words of Mingo County miner J. B. Wiggins, the 'struggle for freedom and liberty.'"

–historian David A. Corbin

REFERENCES

Barkey, Fred A. "The Bull Moose Special." The West Virginia Encyclopedia. January 11, 2011. https://www.wvencyclopedia.org/articles/707.

"Films: The Mine Wars." Public Broadcasting Service, January 26, 2016. http://www.pbs.org/wgbh/americanexperience/features/introduction /minewars-introduction/.

Matewan. "Greed and Destruction in the Mountains." May 18, 2013. https://matewan.wordpress.com/.

Pennsylvania Federation. "Miners Risk Everything to Defend Their Rights." http://www.pennfedbmwe.org/?zone=/unionactive/view_article .cfm&HomeID=95510.

Todd, Roxy. "Do You Know Where the Word 'Redneck' Comes From? Mine Wars Museum Opens, Revives Lost Labor History." West Virginia Public Broadcasting, May 18 2015. http://wvpublic.org/post/do-you -know-where-word-redneck-comes-mine-wars-museum-opens -revives-lost-labor-history#stream/0.

Tyson, Daniel. "Remembering the Violent Coal Wars." *The Register-Herald*, December 5, 2014. http://www.register-herald.com/news /remembering-the-violent-coal-wars/article_8f70204b-634f -5df0-b065-6f5c721deec6.html.

West Virginia Archives and History: "West Virginia's Mine Wars." http://www.wvculture.org/goldenseal/Spring16/BlairMountain.html.

West Virginia Chronicle, Times Dispatch, June 15, 1913. http://virginiachron- icle.com/cgi-bin/virginia?a=d&d=TD19130615.1.39.

West Virginia Division of Culture and History. "Matewan Massacre." West Virginia Archives and History. http://www.wvculture.org/history/labor /matewan04.html.

The West Virginia Mine Wars Museum. "Home." http://www.wvminewars .com/.

"West Virginia Mining." Public Broadcasting Service. http://www.pbs.org /wgbh/americanexperience/features/timeline/minewars/.

12.

TULSA, OKLAHOMA

Ever Heard of "Black Wall Street"?
There's a Reason You Might Not Have

In 1921, the Greenwood District neighborhood of Tulsa, Oklahoma, was the site of one of the most devastating massacres in the entire history of United States. It was a massacre so ghastly it was hidden from textbooks and even oral histories for decades. As we struggle today to understand contemporary violence against African Americans, it's especially important to know this history and to try to understand what happened, and to realize that in the course of just a night or two, that history was brutally stolen from them.

Known as "Black Wall Street" to those in the community, Greenwood in the early part of the twentieth century was a thriving business district featuring African American–owned businesses, a strong Black working class, middle class, and even upper class, with abundant schools, hospitals, and theaters. It was a bustling commercial and social "island" on the northeast side of Tulsa, Oklahoma.

In just two days in the spring of 1921, however, it was all destroyed. Anywhere from fifty-five to three hundred people were killed and eight hundred injured. Many accounts of the demise of Black Wall Street refer to it as a "race riot," but nothing could be further from the truth. It is better described as a terrorist attack on an affluent Black neighborhood. The armed Black men involved were defending their homes, their businesses, and their lives.

Note on photo reads: "All that was left of his home after 'Tulsa Race Riot' 6-1-1921"

WHY TULSA?

Oklahoma, rich in oil deposits, became a state in 1907. It offered a promise of a better life for many formerly enslaved African Americans looking for a chance to start over and get away from the still repressive Southern states.

In Tulsa, the Frisco railroad tracks divided the "white" part of town from the Greenwood District, called "Little Africa." Laws prevented both whites and Blacks from living in neighborhoods that were 75 percent Black or white, respectively, so segregation "naturally" fell into place.

Red brick buildings sprang up along Greenwood Avenue, occupied by businesses owned by a thriving Black middle class that continued to grow during an oil boom in the 1910s. Theaters, nightclubs, churches, and grocery stores thrived in the Greenwood District. The schools were superior to those of the white areas, and many of the houses had indoor plumbing before those in the white areas did.

Because African Americans couldn't shop in areas that were predominantly white, a lot of money spent in Greenwood went right back into the community. By the time of the attacks on the citizens of Black Wall Street, there were more than ten thousand African Americans living in the area. The community supported two of its own newspapers, the Tulsa *Star* and the Oklahoma *Sun*—the latter covering state and national news and politics as well.

But as the community flourished, so did disgruntlement and hatred. The country was still reeling from the defeat of the post–Civil War Reconstruction, and states were furiously enacting Jim Crow laws, which enforced white supremacy and stripped rights from Black Americans. African American men in other parts of the United States had been falsely accused of sexual attacks on white women, and were subsequently put to death—usually at the hands of a lynch mob. The Ku Klux Klan had approximately two thousand members in the Tulsa area by the end of 1921. With veterans returning from World War I and jobs becoming more scarce, envy and racial tension grew among some white citizens of Tulsa.

This all came to a terrifying head on May 31 and June 1, 1921. Over the course of sixteen hours, almost every business—each hotel, both hospitals, libraries, the newspapers, and doctors' offices—was burned to the ground. Police detained and arrested six thousand of the ten thousand African Americans who lived in the Greenwood District. Nine thousand of them were left homeless. Thirty-five city blocks, comprising 1,256 residences, were razed. In today's dollars, it was the equivalent of $30 million in damage; family fortunes vanished overnight.

Estimates of the dead vary, from fifty-five to three hundred. Several prominent Black businessmen and doctors were killed, including A. C. Jackson, recognized as one of the best surgeons of his time by the Mayo brothers, two of Tulsa's most important pioneers. Jackson was shot after he had surrendered to some of the mob to protect his family and was being taken to the jail. Nobody was ever found guilty of his murder.

THE SPARK

It's never been fully settled exactly what happened between a Black man named Dick Rowland, a shoeshine, and Sarah Page, an elevator operator at the Drexel Building in downtown Tulsa, but some of the few people working on May 30, 1921—Memorial Day—reported that they heard a scream and then saw Rowland rushing away from the building. There is speculation that the two were lovers, something that would have gotten both into serious trouble, but nothing was ever con-

Note on photo reads: "'Little Africa on Fire,' Tulsa Race Riot, June 1st, 1921."

firmed. What is clear is that her scream was interpreted as a sign that Rowland "assaulted" her. It was a claim that she denied to the police upon being questioned.

What did happen was that the afternoon paper, the Tulsa *Tribune*, ran the headline, "Nab Negro for Attacking Girl In an Elevator." The local police, aware that such an allegation could mean Rowland would fall victim to a lynch mob, took Rowland into protective custody at the top floor of the Tulsa County Courthouse.

Word spread and soon hundreds of whites gathered outside the courthouse with guns and torches. News of a potential lynching hit the Greenwood District, and several of the Black veterans of World War I who had weapons at home went and gathered them. Thirty African American men headed toward the jail, weapons in hand, intending to prevent Rowland's demise. They offered to help the sheriff defend Rowland from the mob; but he declined—probably aware that the entire scene was about to explode.

And it did. The white mob outside the jail swelled to two thousand, many bringing arms from their houses. More Black men arrived later that evening in automobiles, weapons at the ready. At 10 p.m., in an apparent scuffle between a sheriff's deputy and one of the armed Black men, shots rang out, and then, as many eyewitnesses stated, "All hell broke loose." Soon ten white men and two Black men were lying dead in the street.

The armed Black men backed up to defend Greenwood, but, vastly outnumbered, they took to the heights of nearby buildings and residences and began shooting from above. The mob then began to set fire to the buildings and houses in the Greenwood District and refused to allow firefighters to extinguish the blazes—at gunpoint. Skirmishes, drive-by shootings, and outright murders occurred throughout the night, as more buildings caught fire. Some of Greenwood's African American citizens fled on foot, fearing for their lives.

AFTERMATH

By midday on June 1, all that was left were ashes, bodies, and still-burning neighborhoods. National Guard troops arrived, and with the declaration of martial law, the chaos came to a halt.

Six thousand African American men were rounded up by troops; individuals were released only if they could be vouched for by a white person or employer. The rest were jailed. No white Tulsan was ever arrested or tried. The blame for the destruction was put squarely onto the residents of Greenwood. Much like in Ferguson, Missouri, almost one hundred years later, the Tulsa police department took no responsibility. That said, a few members of the department had put themselves at great risk by keeping Rowland from being lynched.

Even after the embers cooled and the dead were buried the racial violence continued. Tulsa's white leaders worked to keep Greenwood from being resurrected. Ordinances were passed to prevent homes from being rebuilt in the district. There was talk of rebuilding the district as an industrial center and relocating Blacks to an area much further from downtown.

African American lawyers won an injunction to stop that from happening, and many residents did rebuild, although most of them did so without any insurance money, since insurance companies could refuse to pay damages from riots. The rebuilt

Nab Negro for Attacking Girl In an Elevator

A negro delivery boy who gave his name to the police as "Diamond Dick" but who has been identified as Dick Rowland, was arrested on South Greenwood avenue this morning by Officers Carmichael and Pack, charged with attempting to assault the 17-year-old white elevator girl in the Drexel building early yesterday.

He will be tried in municipal court this afternoon on a state charge.

The girl said she noticed the negro a few minutes before the attempted assault looking up and down the hallway on the third floor of the Drexel building as if to see if there was anyone in sight but thought nothing of it at the time.

A few minutes later he entered the elevator she claimed, and attacked her, scratching her hands and face and tearing her clothes. Her screams brought a clerk from Renberg's store to her assistance and the negro fled. He was captured and identified this morning both by the girl and clerk, police say.

Rowland denied that he tried to harm the girl, but admitted he put his hand on her arm in the elevator when she was alone.

Tenants of the Drexel building said the girl is an orphan who works as an elevator operator to pay her way through business college.

SOCIALISTS WIN PLEA

Two Papers are Restored to Mailing Rights

WASHINGTON. — The Milwaukee Leader and the New York Call were restored today to the second class mailing privileges, it was announced by the postoffice department.

WETUMKA MAN NAMED

Tulsa *Tribune*, May 30, 1921

Aftermath of the burning of Black Wall Street

Greenwood District flourished until, in the 1950s, two major interstate highways and "urban renewal" efforts pushed almost all of the Black residents out of the district and further north.

To this day, even including the 1985 MOVE bombing in Philadelphia by police, this remains the single largest massacre of African American citizens in the history of the United States. Black Wall Street stands as just one example of the acts of racist violence that stain our history and have perpetuated racial inequity in the United States.

REFERENCES

Barsocchini, Robert. "1921: Black Business District in Tulsa, Oklahoma, Attacked, Aerially Bombed and Razed, Victims Dumped in Mass Graves." *Washington's Blog*, May 16, 2015. http://www.washingtonsblog.com/2015/05/1921-black -business-district-in-tulsa-oklahoma-attacked-aerially-bombed-and-razed-victims-dumped-in-mass-graves.html.

Bates, Michael. "The 1921 Tulsa Race Riot and the 90 Years that followed." *BatesLine* (Blog), May 30, 2011. http:// www.batesline.com/archives/2011/05/the-1921-tulsa-race-riot-and-the.html.

Bowen, David. "Tulsa's Successful District, 1830–1921." Black Wall Street. http://www.blackwallstreet.org/ourhistory.

Carlson, I. Marc. "Women's Klan in Tulsa." The Tulsa Race Riot of 1921. Updated April 19, 2016. https://tulsaraceriot .wordpress.com/tag/tulsa-tribune/.

Chikwendu, Talibah. "Remembering Black Wall Street." New American Media: African American. Updated on June 8, 2010. http://newamericamedia.org/2010/06/remembering-black-wall-street.php.

Ellsworth, Scott. "Tulsa Race Riot." The Encyclopedia of Oklahoma History and Culture. www.okhistory.org.

Friedersdorf, Conor. "Ferguson's Conspiracy Against Black Citizens." *Atlantic*, March 5, 2015. https://www.theatlantic. com/national/archive/2015/03/ferguson-as-a-criminal-conspiracy-against-its-black-residents-michael-brown -department-of-justice-report/386887/.

Krehbiel, Randy. "The Questions That Remain." Tulsa World. http://www.tulsaworld.com/app/race-riot/timeline.html.

Muhammad, Askia. "Brutal Aftermath of Police MOVE Bombing Still Resonates." *The Final Call*, May 20, 2015. http://www.finalcall.com/artman

/publish/National_News_2/article_102361.shtml.

National Archives. "Oklahoma Statehood: November 16, 1907." The Center for Legislative Archives. Updated August 15, 2016. https://www .archives.gov/legislative/features/oklahoma.

Nowell, Shanedra D. "The 1921 Tulsa Race Riot and Its Legacy: Experiencing Place as Text." Yale-New Haven Teachers Institute. http://teachersinstitute.yale.edu/nationalcurriculum/units/2011 /4/11.04.08.x.html.

O'Dell, Larry. "Ku Klux Klan." The Encyclopedia of Oklahoma History and Culture. www.okhistory.org.

Oklahoma Department of Libraries "The Eruption of Tulsa, Attorney General Civil Case no. 1062." Digital Prairie. Updated September 8, 2006. http://digitalprairie.ok.gov/cdm/compoundobject/collection/race-riot /id/1412.

PBS American Experience: "Reconstruction—The Second Civil War," http://www.pbs.org/wgbh/amex/reconstruction/index.html.

Pickens, Josie. "The Destruction of Black Wall Street." *Ebony*, May 31, 2013. http://www.ebony.com/black-history/the-destruction-of-black-wall -street-405#axzz3zyC6wrNp.

Pilgrim, David. "What was Jim Crow?" Ferris State University: Jim Crow Museum of Racist Memorabilia. http://www.ferris.edu/news/jimcrow/what/.

Sulzberger, A. G. "As Survivors Dwindle, Tulsa Confronts Past." *New York Times*, June 19, 2011. http://www.nytimes.com/2011/06/20/us/20tulsa.html.

Tulsa Historical Society and Museum. "1921 Tulsa Race Riot." Online Exhibits. http://tulsahistory.org/learn/online-exhibits/the-tulsa-race-riot/.

Work, John W. *Ain't No Whistle on This Here Train A' Blowin': An African-American Trilogy.* Houston, TX: Strategic Book Publishing, 2013.

13.

BONUS ARMY

The Great Depression Left WWI Vets with the Short End of the Stick. They Weren't Going to Sit Back and Take It

Veterans frequently risk their lives in the name of their country, but they often end up vulnerable when they return home. At some points in our history, treatment of veterans got so bad that it has led to major political change. That's what happened on July 28, 1932, in Washington, DC, when a confrontation between broke and homeless vets and US military personnel so outraged the public that it swayed a presidential election and had major repercussions for decades.

President Herbert Hoover, a Republican, was faced with an unsightly controversy: thousands of destitute veterans had camped out in the capital, forming one of several "Hooverville" encampments around the country. Hoover ordered the nation's military to march on the veterans, torch their makeshift homes, and run them out of town. His opponent in the coming election, Democrat Franklin Delano Roosevelt, knew the move would incense the public. Upon hearing the news, Roosevelt remarked, "Well, this will elect me."

The clash was one of the darkest chapters in the history of American veterans and still resonates today.

PAY THE BONUS!

When veterans of World War I returned home from the front in 1918–1919, they petitioned Congress to offer some sort of compensation for lost wages; military pay was far below what they could have earned at home in factory work or other jobs. In 1924 Congress passed a law to compensate them, but the certificates issued to the veterans were not payable until 1945—more than twenty years later. Many of them knew that they wouldn't live long enough to even collect.

1932 Bonus Army "Cinderella" stamp

As the grumbles continued among the ranks, the stock market crash of 1929 hit, and the Great Depression was in full swing. Those veterans who couldn't find work became part of the destitute masses who had no money, no food, no jobs, and, in some cases, no homes. At its worst, in 1933, unemployment was 25 percent, and prospects were dim for everyone.

Just the year before, in 1932, it was clear to everyone that things would get worse before they got better. Feeling like they'd been chewed up and spit out by their country after doing what they felt was their duty, seventeen thousand veterans made their way to Washington to set up camp and make their case. They were known as the Bonus Expeditionary Force, later shortened to the Bonus Army.

HOOVERVILLES

The Bonus Army occupied abandoned structures along Pennsylvania Avenue between the Capitol and the White House and set up camp in nearby parks and the Anacostia Flats, a swampland east of the Capitol that had been converted into a park in the early 1900s. Those areas swam with tent cities and even some shacks erected from nearby scrap piles. Such

Bonus Army camp, Anacostia Flats, 1932

encampments were known as shantytowns or "Hoovervilles," after the president who would not meet with them, talk to them, or hear their stories.

These makeshift homes were filled with veterans from the Great War, both Black and white, along with their families. Protesters in Hooverville camps wanted to convince the public to support their cause.

Conditions of the camps were as shipshape as they could muster, and the veterans were highly disciplined, with their own post office, library, and newspaper. It was thought that if they did not keep things clean and organized, the public might go against them.

In fact, that was a risk; the infamous tactic of "red-baiting" was used against them by Hoover and his military commanders. Basically, the Bonus Army and their families were called communists and agitators. It was to no avail, however; these tens of thousands of citizens remained within a stone's throw of the White House—sometimes on the lawn itself—and they continued pushing for relief.

On June 15, 1932, with pressure mounting, the House of Representatives passed the Patman Bonus Bill, which would have taken care of the bonus payments in cash immediately. But in what sounds like something out of today's headlines of partisan politics, the Senate shot it down two days later, by a vote of 62 to 18.

Thousands more veterans headed to Washington in response to the defeat of the legislation to compensate them.

COPS VERSUS VETERANS

Initially, the local police were cooperative and even sympathetic to the vets; their chief, Pelham Glassford, was a World War I veteran himself.

But by the end of July, some of the officialdom in DC had grown weary of the camps and what they represented. On July 28, secretary of war Patrick Hurley ordered police to evacuate the buildings that the veterans occupied. In the skirmish that ensued, two veterans were killed.

Hoover then made the fateful order: the army would rout the veterans from the city entirely.

It was none other than General Douglas MacArthur, with the help of Major Dwight Eisenhower, who removed the 1932 Bonus Army from the city, with an assist from Major George Patton, who was in charge of the cavalry brigade that headed the action. They first cleared the abandoned buildings, then MacArthur made a decision to follow the veterans into the Anacostia Flats.

Hoover, sensing the political catastrophe this entire episode might create, twice sent word to MacArthur not to cross the 11th Street Bridge that led to the flats. MacArthur ignored Hoover's suggestions and moved his troops ahead anyway; the soldiers

Bonus Army camped out on the Capitol lawn

marched on the veterans and their homes, setting the tents and shacks ablaze as they cleared them out.

Tear gas canisters flew ahead of them, bayonets flashed in the sun, a machine-gun brigade brandished its terrifying weapons, and a half dozen tanks lined up behind them for visual reinforcement. It was full-on assault, and it routed the tired residents of Hooverville.

When it was all over, at least one baby died from the tear gas, and one veteran's wife miscarried from the same. Added to this toll were the two veterans killed by police a few days earlier and fifty-four injuries from both skirmishes.

Bonus Army members heading to Washington, DC, atop a freight train, 1932

Almost immediately, MacArthur held a press conference where he tried to perform impromptu damage control, claiming the Bonus Army was composed of revolutionaries and communists and that they had threatened the very institution of government. Hoover's statement the next morning called into question the patriotism and loyalty of the veterans. That was a big mistake, as it didn't work; the general public held the whole episode against Hoover during the presidential elections that year. In newsreels at movie theaters nationwide, a chorus of boos would erupt when news of the military action against veterans hit the screens.

Roosevelt was elected by a massive margin later that year. In addition, the Democrats won significant majorities in both houses of Congress. The country was not only tired of the Great Depression, but the fallout from debacles such as the Bonus Army worked against Hoover and his fellow Republicans as well.

While FDR did not himself publicly support the Bonus Army, he did not forget the political cost exacted by actions such as those perpetrated by Hoover. Soon after his election in 1932, FDR established the Civilian Conservation Corps, which created jobs for twenty-five thousand veterans and other Amer-

Police taking on Bonus Marchers, 1932

icans. Similarly, when a smaller Bonus Army went to DC a year later, rather than send troops, he sent his wife Eleanor to meet with them.

In 1936, Congress passed legislation to honor all bonus payments—nine years early. Ultimately, the plight of veterans led to the Servicemen's Readjustment Act of 1944—known as the GI Bill of Rights—which offered multiple benefits, including college education for veterans, though it was rife with racial bias against African Americans until at least the 1960s.

Politicians risk a lot when they treat veterans with callousness—and worse. When unemployment benefits, food stamps, or other programs that help veterans are slashed, there are ramifications; and when deplorable conditions at VA hospitals are brought to light, it casts a shadow on whatever administration is in power at the time.

The story of the Bonus Army should make politicians more compassionate when it comes to veterans' issues, but it shouldn't have to come to that. Veterans—like everyone else—have a right to a good home and a good job in the United States of America.

REFERENCES

Brennan, Linda Crotta. *Franklin D. Roosevelt's Presidency*. Minneapolis, MN: Lerner Publications, 2017.

Delaney, David G. "Bonus Bill (1924)." Major Acts of Congress. Encyclopedia.com. October 1, 2017. http://www.encyclopedia.com/history/encyclopedias-almanacs-transcripts-and-maps/bonus-bill-1924.

EyeWitness to History. "The Bonus Army." http://www.eyewitnesstohistory.com/snprelief4.htm.

Kingseed, Wyatt. "The 'Bonus Army' War in Washington." *American History* (June 2014). http://www.historynet.com

Shacks erected by the Bonus Army, 1932. The Capitol dome is in the background

/the-bonus-army-war-in-washington.htm.

Schmidt, Hans. *Maverick Marine: General Smedley D. Butler and the Contradictions of American Military History*. Lexington: University Press of Kentucky, 2014.

Speakman, Joseph M. "Into the Woods: The First Year of the Civilian Conservation Corps." *Prologue* 38, no. 3 (Fall 2006). https://www.archives.gov/publications/prologue/2006/fall/ccc.html.

Watkins, Thayer. "The Great Depression of the 1930s and Its Origins." San Jose State University. http://www.sjsu.edu/faculty/watkins/dep1929.htm.

Z., Mickey. "The Bonus Army." Zinn Education Project. Teaching *A People's History*. https://zinnedproject.org/materials/the-bonus-army/.

14.

THE MINNEAPOLIS GENERAL STRIKE OF 1934

It Began with Truck Drivers Who Wanted a Union. They Became Teamsters

Traditional unions or workers' groups in Minneapolis in 1934 were a little stodgy, didn't push too hard for workers' rights, and were happy maintaining the status quo.

Enter Teamsters Local 574. It was the kind of union that felt the strong need to include inside workers as well as truck drivers and helpers as members. A union organizing drive was conducted by people who worked in the trade, some of whom subscribed to a leftist political philosophy that put them in hyper-organizing mode in early 1934. Their approach worked for coal drivers, whose strike was settled quickly in February, and the ranks of Local 574 swelled immediately after. The workers who spearheaded the strike organizing were Carl Skoglund and the three Dunn brothers: Grant, Miles, and Vince. They were joined by Farrell Dobbs, a key strike leader among the rank and file. As a result, the self-confidence of the rank and file also grew.

As they prepared for the expected general strike after pushback from trucking companies, they created a commissary, garage, and an infirmary, and they mobilized a ladies' auxiliary that included members' wives. Some wives even played a part in the street fighting with cops that was to come.

Ladies' auxiliary unit. Image courtesy of International Brotherhood of Teamsters Archives. Used with permission

They were ready. In late April, the union demanded recognition, closed shops (where only Teamster members could work), shorter hours, and a pay scale that was citywide, rather than different wages set by each employer.

The trucking companies had been organized for thirty-five years via the Citizens Alliance, an employer-funded and -supported group that included well-heeled local property owners as well as politically right-wing individuals. It was staunchly antiunion and often resorted to violence to achieve its ends. The cops were also strong supporters of the Citizens Alliance.

You can see where this is going.

By May, with Local 574 swelling to five thousand members but still several of the trucking companies refusing to recognize the fledgling union, a general drivers' strike was called for the city of Minneapolis.

Trucks that normally moved freight and goods around the city every day suddenly halted. The strikers used some innovative techniques, such as "flying pickets"—squads of members with their own trucks, emblazoned with a special union sign to prevent confusion, would patrol the city to ensure no scab trucks were moving freight.

Other tactics were successful as well; a daily newspaper, called *The Organiser*, kept the commu-

A "flying picket" truck carrying strikers.
Image courtesy of International Brotherhood of Teamsters Archives.
Used with permission

nity and the members informed. A committee of one hundred members across jurisdictions and companies coordinated efforts to supply food and resources to strikers and their families.

Another innovative technique was to develop ties with the unemployed people in the community; they were a potential source of scab drivers for the employers. That threat was neutralized, and the unemployed were firmly on the side of the strikers.

Three days after the strike began, the first wave of violence erupted, and it kept up for another three days. It was instigated by the company goons, via the Citizens Alliance and the police who favored (and basically worked for) them.

One of the final battles involved twenty thousand strikers versus cops and members of the Citizens Alliance, and it galvanized the workers involved, as well as thirty-four thousand city workers who saw what was happening and walked out of their jobs in solidarity.

The strikers had forced the employers' hand, and agreements were reached that basically gave them what they wanted. On paper, anyway. In reality, the companies did not live up to their part of the bargain, ignoring some of the agreements and firing some of the most active union supporters as well. The tentative truce did not hold up.

Not two months later, on July 17, the strike resumed. The Citizens Alliance, however, had plans to disrupt it. Luring strikers into a corner by sending a scab truck through their lines, one hundred cops fired directly into a large group of unarmed men, killing two and injuring sixty-five—many of whom were shot in the back. That day was known from then on as "Bloody Friday."

Public outcry was loud and effective; unions from all over the country sent donations and food, and all city transport workers staged a one-day strike.

One hundred thousand people showed up at the funeral of

Funeral procession for Henry Ness. Image courtesy of International Brotherhood of Teamsters Archives. Used with permission

Henry Ness, one of the strikers killed on Bloody Friday.

As frequently happens in situations like these, the governor stepped in, declared martial law, and sent four thousand National Guard soldiers to keep things from escalating—in other words, to help break the strike. They assisted in ushering scab trucks to their destinations. Picketing was banned.

Another general strike was called for August 1, in direct defiance of martial law and the governor. In response, the troops were sent to union headquarters to arrest as many of the union leaders as they could find. This enraged union members and their supporters even more, and forty thousand of them marched to the stockade where their comrades were being held, demanding their release. They were indeed set free, and the union headquarters office was returned to Local 574 from the hands of the guardsmen.

In the end, the powerful Citizens Alliance had been broken, the employers agreed to the union's major demands, including wage increases, union protection in their existing workplaces ("barns," they're sometimes called—a throwback to when Teamsters drove horse-drawn wagons rather than trucks), and a recognition that the union could and would organize inside workers, as well as others across jurisdictions. Minneapolis had become a union town, and it still has a strong Teamster presence today, all across the state.

Last, this kind of violence against workers trying to join a union was one of the main arguments in favor of the National Labor Relations Act, guaranteeing workers the right to organize and bargain, which was made into law in July 1935.

REFERENCES

Alam, Ehsan. "Minneapolis Teamsters' Strike, 1934." Minnesota Historical Society: MNOPedia. http://www.mnopedia.org/event /minneapolis-teamsters-strike-1934.

International Brotherhood of Teamsters. "1934 Minnesota Strike." Teamster History. https://teamster.org/about/teamster-history/1934.

International Brotherhood of Teamsters. "Today in 1934: Minneapolis Teamsters Vote to Strike All Trucking Companies." Teamster History. https://teamster.org/blog/2015/11/today-1934-minneapolis-teamsters -vote-strike-all-trucking-companies-0.

Roper, Eric. "Plaque Will Mark Bloody Battle of 1934 Truckers' Strike in Minneapolis." *Star Tribune* (Blog), June 22, 2015. http://www .startribune.com/plaque-will-mark-bloody-battle-of-1934-truckers -strike-in-minneapolis/308195201/.

Battle, strike 1934

National Guard troops keeping a crowd back during a raid on strike headquarters in Minneapolis, 1934. Image via Minnesota Historical Society

15.

SITTING DOWN, STRIKING FLINT

These Images Might Look Like Some Lazy Workers,
Up to No Good. But They're Actually Heroes

The United Auto Workers (UAW) was formed in 1935, about the same time the National Labor Relations Act (NLRA) was made into law. The NLRA was Washington's way of getting some labor peace after decades of struggle that at times got violent. It more or less made it clear that unions could, in fact, organize—legally.

The UAW had previously held strikes in various small plants, but after the NLRA was enacted, the union made a conscious decision to go after a huge target—the biggest and most powerful, in fact. General Motors (GM) was the choice.

ON THE JOB

The issues that affected autoworkers, especially at the plants the UAW chose, were as follows:

- Deadly working conditions. On-the-job injuries ended with the workers cast aside like scrap metal, with no compensation for injuries. There wasn't even a medical station in the plant. As one of the people who worked there said later, "There wasn't a man coming out of that mill without having a couple fingers cut off."

- Frenetic assembly line speeds. Sometimes they were so fast that workers actually passed out. And nothing—not even a death or injury—would stop the lines.

- No vacation time, no overtime pay, no sick days, and no workers' compensation. And you could be fired for any reason at all, or laid off for months without pay because they were changing models.

- No breaks. In the summer of 1936, which had a heat wave of sorts, this was especially a problem; hundreds died on the line at various plants due to heat exhaustion.

This strike was not about money; it was about humane treatment on the job and recognition of the union.

TARGET LOCKED: FISHER BODY PLANT #2

The union identified two targets: a plant in Flint, Michigan, that produced dies from which car parts were stamped, and a similar plant in Cleveland, Ohio. If they could control the means of production, the rest would fall into place.

One of the biggest of GM's plants was the production complex in Flint. The town was pretty much owned by GM. In fact, when one of the organizers checked into his hotel room, a phone call came for him within minutes; the anonymous caller told him to get out of town or he'd be "carried out in a wooden box." The wheels were in motion for the UAW to strike the GM Fisher body plant #2 in Flint.

Sit-down strikers guarding the window entrance to Fisher body plant #3, 1937

IT BEGINS

Events changed that plan—or, rather, accelerated it—when two brothers were fired at the Cleveland Fisher body plant, which happened to be the second primary UAW target, and the rest of the workers there spontaneously walked out in support. The UAW saw an opportunity. It declared it wouldn't settle things in Cleveland without getting a national contract covering all of GM's plants.

Meanwhile, GM was planning to move machinery out of the Flint plant in anticipation of what was coming. The workers acted swiftly and decisively, and in an historic move, on December 30, 1936, they simply stopped working and sat down. Soon, other plants joined the strikes.

In all, tens of thousands of workers eventually joined the actions.

So began the sit-down strikes that would define the UAW for generations to come. Until that point, strikes were usually done outside facilities; the sit-down was a relatively new tactic, and it worked because it kept management and strikebreakers from entering the plant. Production came to a screeching halt, at a time when demand for automobiles was high.

GOVERNMENT OF THE PEOPLE, BY THE PEOPLE

The workers had their own system of governance, including a mayor, and departments such as postal service, sanitation, organized recreation, information, and even a kind of "court" system. Many of the rank-and-file workers who led the strike in Flint were members of the Socialist and Communist parties, which meant they were highly organized and understood the need for struggle. The Women's Emergency Brigade, composed of striking workers' wives, was key to helping build and sustain support for the strike. This was a highly coordinated strike, and it needed to be.

GM used every tactic it could to force the strikers out of the plant, including cutting electricity, heat, and food. Support for the strikers grew in the community—outside vendors provided food, and a sympathetic local restaurant served up meals for all two thousand strikers each day. The strikers' lives were intertwined with those of the community and small businesses around the plants, and that meant a sort of natural David and Goliath situation, with GM as the giant to be slayed.

QUICK, SEND IN THE COPS. DON'T BOTHER, THEY'RE HERE . . .

As in many strikes at the time, GM arranged for the police to try to get the strikers out of the plant. Strikers met them with fire hoses and car parts, keeping the cops at bay for hours. When police hurled tear gas into the building, the Women's Emergency Brigade smashed the windows to let air into the factory.

It got to a point that Washington was summoned to break the strike. Though vice president John Nance Garner was in favor, president Franklin D. Roosevelt refused to break the strike, instead asking GM to settle and recognize the union.

After pressuring local and district judges, GM received a court injunction against the strikers. The UAW ignored that and instead occupied another local plant to force GM's hand. As negotiations began between the UAW and GM, the Michigan National Guard was called in to keep the peace, by preventing police, workers, and strikebreakers alike from entering the plants. The workers refused to yield.

It worked; the strike lasted forty-four days, and it showed that workers' power could be used to bring a giant to its knees. A contract was signed, and the UAW's reputation was sealed. In the next year, membership grew from thirty thousand to half a million. This was a victory for working people worldwide. In fact, the BBC later declared it "The Strike Heard Round The World."

National Guard with machine guns, overlooking Chevrolet plants # 9 and # 4

REFERENCES

BBC. "The 1936-1937 Flint, Michigan Sit-Down Strike." http://www.bbc
.co.uk/dna/place-london/A672310.

Carmody, Steve. "Flint Sit-Down Strike—75 Years Later." Michigan Radio,
December 30, 2011. http://michiganradio.org/post/flint-sit-down-
strike-75-years-later.

College of Charleston, "The Flint Sit-Down Strike, 1937." https://blogs
.cofc.edu/palmettoprogram/files/2015/02/The-Flint-Sit-Down-Strike
-1937-1qtt5ga.pdf.

Eller, Troy. "Subject Focus: Remembering the Sit-Down," (blog), Wayne State University, Walter Reuther Library, December 17, 2010. https://reuther.wayne.edu/node/7092.

Encyclopedia Britannica. "United Automobile Workers (UAW)." January 17, 2011. https://www.britannica.com/topic/United -Automobile-Workers.

Fine, Sydney. *Sit-Down: The General Motors Strike of 1936–1937*. Ann Arbor: University of Michigan Press, 1969.

Harrison, Jon. "February 11, 1937: General Motors Recognizes UAW." *Red Tape* (Blog), Michigan State University, February 11, 2017. https:// blogs.lib.msu.edu /red-tape/2017/feb/february-11-1937-general-motors-recognizes-uaw/.

History.com. "Flint Sit-Down Strike Begins." This Day in History, 2010. http://www .history.com/this-day-in-history/sit-down-strike-begins-in-flint.

Murray, Joshua, and Michael Schwartz. "Moral Economy, Structural Leverage, and Organizational Efficacy: Class Formation and the Great Flint Sit-Down Strike, 1936–1937." *Critical Historical Studies* 2, no. 2 (Fall 2015): 219–259.

Parshall, Lorene. "Remembering Iconic Flint Sit-Down Strike of 1937." *Petoskey News*, January 31, 2012. http://articles.petoskeynews.com/2012-01-31/support -strikers_31011016.

Virginia Polytechnic Institute. "Which Side Are You On? The Flint Sit-Down Strike of 1936–1937." Digital History Reader. http://www.dhr. history.vt.edu/modules/us /mod06_1936/context.html.

16.

THE BATTLE OF THE OVERPASS

*A PR Disaster for Ford Motor Company
that Kick-Started the UAW*

n 1937, things were hot as molten iron in and around Detroit when it came to unionizing autoworkers. The National Labor Relations Act, established in 1935, gave workers a lot more rights when it came to organizing, and it included the right to distribute information at the gates of factories to get out the truth about what it meant to join a union and gain workers' rights. The UAW had seen some recent big successes at Chrysler and GM and was gaining ground with Ford, but the latter company fought hard against letting the union in.

One of the key events that turned the tide, at Ford's massive River Rouge plant in Dearborn, Michigan, has been known ever since as the Battle of the Overpass. On May 26, 1937, the UAW decided to take action with an informational flyer-and-newsletter campaign talking about the newly won rights under the NLRA as well as a campaign to raise wages from $6 for an eight-hour workday ($99 in today's dollars) to $8 for a six-hour workday ($132 today).

Sure, they were shooting high, but it was designed to get attention—and to get Ford talking. The River Rouge plant, one of the largest of its kind in the world, had nine thousand workers that the UAW wanted to reach.

After many workers took the flyers that the roughly forty organizers had been passing out all day

Ford Workers

UNIONISM NOT FORDISM

Now is the time to Organize!
The Wagner Bill is behind you!
Now get behind yourselves!

General Motors Workers, Chrysler Workers, Briggs Workers have won higher wages and better working conditions. 300,000 automobile workers are marching forward under the banner of the United Automobile Workers Union.

JOIN NOW IN THE MARCH AND WIN:

Higher Wages and Better Working Conditions
Stop Speed-up by Union Supervision
6 Hour Day, 8 Dollars Minimum Pay
Job Security thru Seniority Rights
End the Ford Service System
Union Recognition

Organize and be Recognized - JOIN NOW!

Union Headquarters
for Ford Workers:
} Michigan Avenue at Addison
Vernor Highway West, and Lawndale

Sign up at Union Headquarters for Ford Workers or at any office of the United Automobile Workers

1324 Clay at Russell	8944 Jos. Campau at Playfair
2441 Milwaukee at Chene	11440 Charlevoix at Gladwin
11725 Oakland at Tuxedo	1343 East Ferry at Russell
4044 Leuschner at Dwyer	3814—35th Street at Michigan
11640 East Jefferson	2730 Maybury Grand at Michigan
10904 Mack at Lemay	4715 Hastings Street
77 Victor at John R.	Room 509 Hofmann Bldg.

Distributed by
United Automobile Workers of America

License No. 4

Printed by Goodwill Printing Co.
33

Original flyer passed out at the gate, Ford River Rouge plant, 1937. Image via Walter P. Reuther Library

Opposite: The Ford-hired thugs arrive. Reuther is third from the right. Image via Walter P. Reuther Library

long, UAW organizers Walter Reuther, Richard Frankensteen, and two more gathered on the pedestrian overpass over Miller Road at gate 4 of the plant for photos by *Detroit News* photographer James R. "Scotty" Kilpatrick. The Ford logo was behind them, which is why they chose that spot.

It was a fateful decision.

Private security guards from Ford came out (by some estimates, as many as forty) and attacked them. The organizers were beaten, kicked, thrown down stairs (breaking the back of one of the men), and slammed into the ground. The photographer was also accosted by the guards, who demanded he turn over the photographic plates to them so they could be destroyed. In a brilliant move, he hid the actual plates under the seat of his car and gave them blanks.

This turned out to be a crucial decision. After the battle was over, Ford immediately began to spin the incident to make itself look like the victim. The head of security for Ford, Harry Bennett, told *Time* magazine that the "affair was deliberately provoked by union officials . . . they simply wanted to provoke a charge of Ford brutality. . . . I know definitely no Ford service man or plant police were involved in any way in the fight."

But as soon as Kilpatrick's photographs were developed, they hit the presses, and the tide turned quickly when newspapers all over the country featured the brutality of Ford's hired goons. Public opinion was firmly on the side of the workers.

In fact, when Henry Ford's lawyers and Bennett were called in front of the newly established National Labor Relations Board on violating the National Labor Relations Act in dozens of ways, members of the press—such as Kilpatrick—gave the most damning evidence, along with Ford workers, who testified that if anybody who worked in the belly of the Ford beast expressed an interest at all in unionizing, they were fired immedi-

ately and escorted out of the plant.

All of this happened in 1937, and Henry Ford finally realized he had to recognize the union and negotiate a contract.

Four years later, the UAW finally had its first collective bargaining agreement with Ford. The combined one-two punch of the publicity around the Battle of the Overpass and the National Labor Relations Board hearings gave Ford no alternative.

The UAW went on to help create good union jobs and,

Above: The battle begins. Image via Walter P. Reuther Library

eventually, help millions of people achieve a middle-class income with health insurance and pensions as well. Its peak membership was 1.5 million in 1979.

What can we learn from this?

In 1937, these workers fought for an increase in wages to make better lives for their families and their communities. They gave their blood, and sometimes their very lives, in order to make sure future generations had it better than they did. We're at a turning point in this country. Unions now represent a historically low number of working people while income inequality is at one of the most extreme levels ever. These two facts are related.

It's time we rebuilt the labor movement and turned it into the force for good jobs and a thriving middle class that it once was.

REFERENCES

Burcar, Colleen. *It Happened in Michigan: Remarkable Events That Shaped History*. Lanham, MD: Rowman & Littlefield Publishers, 2011.

King, Gilbert. "How the Ford Motor Company Won a Battle and Lost Ground." *Smithsonian*, April 30, 2013. http://www.smithsonianmag.com/history/how-the-ford-motor-company-won-a-battle-and-lost-ground-45814533/.

National Labor Relations Board. "National Labor Relations Act." https://www.nlrb.gov/resources/national-labor-relations-act.

Snavely, Brent. "UAW membership tops 400,000 for the first time since 2008." *USA Today*, March 31, 2015. http://www.usatoday.com/story/money/cars/2015/03/31/uaw-membership-tops-first-time-since/70753012/.

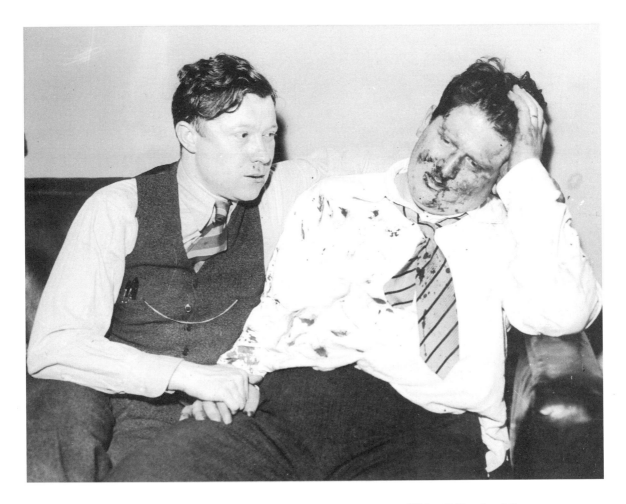

Walter P. Reuther comforts a badly beaten Richard Frankensteen. Image via Walter P. Reuther Library

17.

"ROSIE THE RIVETER"

Remember the "Rosie the Riveter" Image
Pretty Much Everybody Knows? (Ahem)

Rosie the Riveter was a figure that made it into at least one popular song, the cover of a *Saturday Evening Post*, the modern feminist movement, and the very cultural fabric of our country. Like many things, her actual appearance was different from what the media portrayed. Because so many have attempted to claim that they were the model for the "real" Rosie, the truth is still elusive, but we can distill what it was that made Rosie somehow real for Americans—and the world.

The truth is, Rosie the Riveter was not really just one person. She was a composite of the women who went to work, many for the first time, during World War II. These were jobs that had previously been reserved for men—in factories, on assembly lines, welding, driving taxicabs, managing small businesses, and much more. Six million women became Rosies all over the country; from 1940 to 1945, the female workforce grew by 50 percent. The phenomenon even created a secondary demand for childcare workers, as before this childcare had been reserved almost solely for the wealthy.

By 1944, the number of working American women had increased to more than 20 million. Some were of African American descent, some Latina, and other ethnicities that were previously underrepresented in the workforce.

Rosie the Riveter first came into our nation's consciousness by means of a popular song. The effort to recruit women was being spun up as World War II saw more and more men going overseas. In 1942, Redd Evans and John Jacob Loeb penned a song, "Rosie the Riveter," about these women who were going to work in massive numbers. It was later recorded by several different artists and made famous by James Kern "Kay" Kyser.

Then, Norman Rockwell painted this famous cover for the May 29, 1943, edition of the *Saturday Evening Post*. The model he used, Mary Doyle Keefe, died in 2015. Note how muscular and rugged she looks; it's a pretty stark difference between that and what has more recently become the popular image of Rosie the Riveter.

In 1942, J. Howard Miller created the now famous poster for Westinghouse Co., which actually wasn't meant to be Rosie the Riveter, though it was meant to help the war effort as a morale booster.

It wasn't until the early 1980s that this image became what most of us now think of as Rosie the Riveter. It was more or less adopted by the feminist movement, and it remains a popular symbol of women's power.

The fact that women entered the workforce in record numbers during World War

Women operating industrial equipment during World War II

II didn't change the sexist attitudes of the times, however. The average pay for a man working in a wartime plant was $54.65 a week. For women? $31.21.

Even though the war eventually ended and many of those servicemen returned to their old jobs, meaning that many women lost their industrial positions, this marked a turning point: women had proved themselves in the workforce, and many of them didn't want to go back to being dependent on men for their income.

REFERENCES

Brock, Julia, Jennifer W. Dickey, Richard J. W. Harker, and Catherine M. Lewis, eds. *Beyond Rosie: A Documentary History of Women and World War II*. Fayetteville: University of Arkansas Press, 2015.

Metropolitan State University of Denver. "Women & World War II." https://msudenver.edu/camphale/thewomensarmycorps/womenwwii/.

Strobel, Heidi A. "Rosie the Riveter, Rose Will Monroe, and Rose Bonavita." *American National Biography Online* Feb. 2000. http://www.anb.org/articles/20/20-01920.html.

Original *Saturday Evening Post* cover by Norman Rockwell

Westinghouse poster, 1942

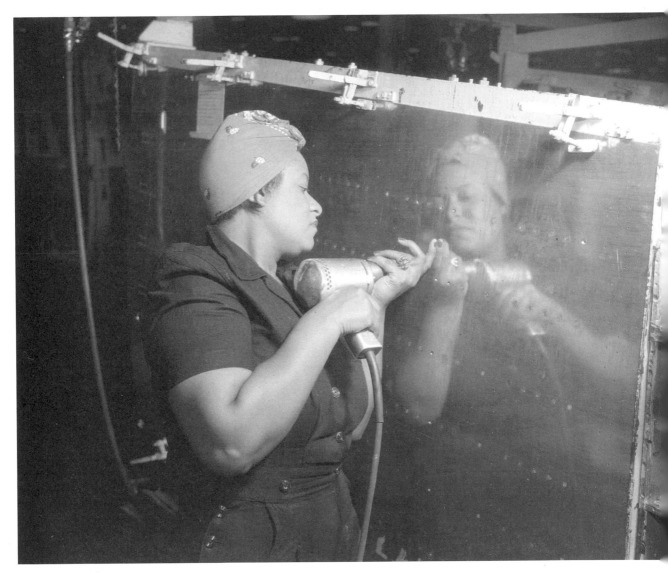

Many "Rosies" were Black women, including this drill operator on the A-31 Vengeance bomber, 1943

18.

UNITED FARMWORKERS

That Time When 14 Million Americans Stopped Eating Grapes, Because Farmworkers Asked Them To

A Latina woman named Dolores Huerta was the seed and a good part of the powerhouse behind what eventually became the United Farmworkers union, which made huge improvements to the lives of largely migrant farmworkers who worked the fields of California and, eventually, those of many other states.

In the early 1950s, Huerta earned a college degree and then began teaching elementary school in Stockton, California, where she saw that her students, mostly children of farmworkers, were living in poverty, without enough food or other basic necessities of life. She became one of the founders of the Community Service Organization in Stockton, which was instrumental in beginning to improve conditions for farmworkers and to fight discrimination. It also helped people fill out tax forms, get children into schools, and study for citizenship.

Also active in this effort were Gilbert Padilla and Cesar Chávez. Chávez was active in organizing area workers to become more politically engaged and try to improve their working conditions. The combination of Huerta's organizing and negotiating skills and the talents of Chávez, especially his dynamic leadership and public speaking prowess, made them nearly unstoppable. They formed the National Farm Workers Association (NFWA).

Cesar Chávez (on the right), speaking at a rally in 1974

One of the key tactics to their success was going door to door and holding house meetings, which connected people in community-based, intimate ways.

It worked.

The big event that birthed the United Farm Workers was in 1965, when Filipino workers at Delano table grape growers struck, and the NFWA, who were mostly of Mexican descent, voted to join them. It was a rare instance of unity among two separate groups of workers with distinctly different heritages. They knew that employers often pitted workers in one area and type of farming against another whenever they demanded better wages and job conditions, so it was a prime opportunity for solidarity among the ranks.

Cesar Chávez

This was also a critical time to use the tactic of community support to rally people who lived in the same areas as the farmworkers, especially considering the political and financial resources that the grape growers would use against the workers.

But what also helped immensely was the use of nonviolence as both a tactic and a moral principle to guide them.

What ultimately got a national stage for the workers was a march, or *peregrinación*, from Delano to Sacramento, the state capital—a march of three hundred miles. With each town came a new crowd of supporters and new media attention. The action ended when one of the smaller grape growers agreed to recognize the NFWA in order to get away from the spotlight. Soon after, the NFWA merged with the UFW, and history was made.

The national grape boycott was called in 1968, and at its peak, more than 17 million Americans had joined in the refusal to buy California grapes. A hunger strike by Chávez brought thousands of farm workers out to see him daily and to the evening religious masses. His action solidified their resolve and captured media attention. Senator Robert Kennedy came out to meet Chávez in a much-publicized trip; it was on this journey that Kennedy announced he was running for president. Sadly, he was assassinated just a few months later.

With the combination of public awareness of the grape boycott and support from other unions like the United Auto Workers (UAW) and American Federation of State, County, and Municipal Employees (AFSCME), which provided financial assistance to the strikers, Delano finally came to the table in 1969 and agreed to a new contract. The boycott had been extremely effective, but it was over.

The settlement provided a number of things that these workers had been seeking for decades:

- An end to the abusive system of "labor contracting," which meant jobs could be assigned by favoritism and bribery. Now, they had a hiring hall, with guaranteed seniority and hiring rights

- Protection from the pesticides that had sickened and killed many farmworkers

- Wage increases

- Fresh water and toilets in the fields (previously scarce commodities)

- A medical plan so farmworkers could access health benefits

In 1972, the United Farm Workers union was officially accepted into the AFL-CIO, an umbrella organization designed to unite many different unions into a federation. A movie about

Dolores Huerta, Image from Walter P. Reuther Library, Wayne State University

Flag and logo of the UFW

the UFW and Cesar Chávez was released in 2014, and *Dolores*, a film about Dolores Huerta, premiered in late 2017.

REFERENCES

Carpenter, Lindsay and Maurice Weeks. "U.S. Farmworkers in California Campaign for Economic Justice (Grape Strike), 1965–70." Swarthmore College: Global Nonviolent Action Database. Updated August 14, 2008. http://nvdatabase.swarthmore.edu/content/us-farmworkers-california-campaign-economic-justice-grape-strike-1965-70.

Dolores Huerta Foundation. "Dolores Huerta." http://doloreshuerta.org/dolores-huerta/.

Garcia, Matt. "Cesar Chavez and the United Farm Workers Movement." *Oxford Research Encyclopedia of American History*. http://americanhistory.oxfordre.com/view/10.1093/acrefore/9780199329175.001.0001/acrefore-9780199329175-e-217.

Tavaana. "Fighting for Farm Workers' Rights: Cesar Chavez, The Delano Grape Strike and Boycott." https://tavaana.org/en/content/fighting-farm-workers-rights-cesar-chavez-delano-grape-strike-and-boycott.

University of San Diego Library. "Forty Acres Delano: United Farm Workers." Farmworker Movement Documentation Project. https://libraries.ucsd.edu/farmworkermovement/category/commentary/forty-acres-delano-united-farm-workers/.

Farmworkers continue to organize to improve their communities and their lives. Here, a child rallies in support of the Coalition of Immokalee Workers, a human rights organization

19.

THE STONEWALL REBELLION

A Civil Rights Battle for the Times

In the 1950s and '60s, being gay was considered un-American. Funny how that term, un-American, is so often used to try and scare people away from gaining their rights, isn't it?

Those were hard times for gay and transgender people in the United States. Their activities were being monitored by government organizations such as the State Department, with the US Post Office, the FBI, and local police departments also involved.

Police would raid gay bars or places "suspected" of having a large number of gay customers. They would show up without warning and then shut them down, and photos of the people they rounded up would be plastered all over the newspapers. Some gay and trans folks were even taken to and "lodged" in mental hospitals, perhaps never being heard from again—when the state or feds committed someone to a facility, there was no escape without extreme efforts on their behalf. As recently as the 1940s, some gay people were subjected against their will to electro-shock treatments, castration, and even lobotomies.

But as of the 1960s, the civil rights movement, along with the antiwar movement, had begun to inspire people to "fight the power," and this gained momentum across several layers of our society. Folks were rebelling against arbitrary police actions that kept citizens intimidated and in the shadows when they tried to rise up. There was a full-blown cultural shift happening—people were simply not going to live with the rigid social constructs of the 1950s anymore.

This was the setting, then, for the rebellion that launched the modern gay rights movement, beginning on June 28, 1969, in a Greenwich Village, New York City, bar called Stonewall Inn.

It was a popular hangout for gay and trans people in the area—an oasis, as many gay bars in the area had been shut down by the local police. At the time of the rebellion, it was one of the only bars in Manhattan that allowed people to slow dance with one another regardless of gender identity or orientation. That alone was revolutionary.

To prevent the frequent raids that targeted their patrons, bar owners had to pay off cops—but that didn't always stop them. Some say the owners of Stonewall Inn, who were members of the powerful Genovese Mafia family, paid off cops in order to provide liquor sales without a license and to stave off raids. To this day, it's not clear whether police raided Stonewall Inn on June 28 in spite of being paid off or because they actually hadn't been paid off on this particular occasion.

Unbelievably, during such raids, women were escorted to the restroom so female cops could "verify their sex." Anybody who was there without ID was arrested, as was anyone not wearing three pieces of clothing "appropriate" for their apparent sex. All liquor was usually confiscated, too.

This had been pretty standard for gay bars since the 1950s, but something was different that night in June. The people fought back.

About two hundred people at the Stonewall Inn that night refused to comply with police demands to show their IDs and to "prove" their sex. However, this time, those not arrested or sent into the street didn't disperse as usual. They hung around outside the bar to see what was going to happen next. More

Stonewall Inn, 1969

Gay Liberation Front demonstration, 1972

people came from the surrounding neighborhood, swelling the crowd to several hundred, and even more arrived as word went out about the raid. The neighborhood's population was not going to be compliant tonight.

As cops escorted more patrons out of the bar, some began to shout "Gay power!" and to sing "We Shall Overcome," the song adopted by civil rights demonstrators all over the country. It was totally appropriate. Laughter soon turned to rage, and the air was electric with rebellion and resistance.

Coins, followed by beer bottles and eventually rocks, were thrown at the police and their vehicles as rumors spread among the growing crowd that some inside the bar were being beaten.

It's unknown what the true catalyst was, but as the story goes, it was likely after one too many rough arrests that the crowd couldn't take it anymore, and the situation ignited. All police vehicles immediately sped away for fear of being overturned. Some cops remained, grabbing a few of the citizens and observers on hand—including a journalist and a musician, possibly as "impartial" witnesses—and retreating back into the bar for safety.

The following hour saw rocks, bricks, and garbage cans thrown at the door of the bar, windows broken, and some fires set.

By the time the fire trucks made it, the cops had managed to get themselves out of the bar without incident. Then came the tactical police force. Imagine the riot-gear-wearing, jack-booted cops like the ones who tear-gassed Occupy Wall Street folks several years ago. Or like those more recently in Baltimore or Ferguson. This was the precursor to that style of riot "control," and they'd perfected their tactics against the civil rights demonstrations and antiwar actions earlier in the decade.

What followed totally infuriated the cops in riot formation. The crowd formed Rockettes-style chorus kick lines, dancing and making fun of the cops, singing these words to the tune of

> Now, times were a-changin'. Tuesday night was the last night for bullshit. . . . Predominantly, the theme was, "This shit has got to stop!"
> —Anonymous Stonewall riots participant

"The Howdy Doody Show" theme song:

We are the Stonewall girls
We wear our hair in curls
We don't wear underwear
We show our pubic hair
We wear our dungarees
Above our Nelly knees!

As Martin Duberman wrote in his 1993 book, *Stonewall*, "It was a deliciously witty, contemptuous counterpoint to the [police]'s brute force."

This humiliation only increased the savagery of the cops, who charged again and again, batons swinging. The crowd and kick lines would disperse as the riot formation advanced and re-form after it had passed, resuming their impromptu performances and taunting the cops further—from behind, forcing the cops themselves to turn around and re-form before they began another attack. Even when police managed to capture some of the demonstrators, people in the crowd would give chase and pull their comrades from their grasp rather than let them be beaten and thrown into police trucks.

Poet Allen Ginsberg, who lived in Greenwich Village and visited Stonewall during one of the nights of the rebellion, stated admiringly: "You know, the guys there were so beautiful—they've lost that wounded look that fags all had ten years ago." (Note that the term "fags" as used here was not derogatory when used by somebody within the community at the time.)

The Stonewall Rebellion lasted for five days before subsiding. Its effect, however, was permanent. A year later, a march was held in Greenwich Village to remember Stonewall. Los Angeles and Chicago held simultaneous marches. These were the first gay pride marches in the history of the United States, and from

"Part of history forgets that as the cops are inside the bar, the confrontation started outside by throwing change at the police. We started with the pennies, the nickels, the quarters, and the dimes. 'Here's your payoff, you pigs! You fucking pigs! Get out of our faces.' This was started by the street queens of that era."
–Sylvia Rivera, transgender activist and cofounder, Gay Liberation Front and the Gay Activists Alliance

Images from PBS *American Experience: The Stonewall Riots Explained*

those grew thousands more in cities and towns all across the country.

It also sparked the formation of many gay and trans rights groups, and is regarded as a turning point in the US gay liberation movement itself.

REFERENCES

Baruch College. "New York City (NYC): Stonewall Inn Riot—1969." Disasters. http://www.baruch.cuny.edu/nycdata/disasters/riots-stonewall.html.

Carter, David. *Stonewall: The Riots That Sparked the Gay Revolution*. New York: St. Martin's Press, 2004.

Daigle, Robert. "Stonewall: The Lost Chapter of Modern History." NU Writing. http://www.northeastern.edu/nuwriting/stonewall-the-lost-chapter-of-modern-history/.

Duberman, Martin. *Stonewall*. New York: Plume, 1994.

Molloy, Parker Marie. "Op-ed: Happy Birthday, Sylvia Rivera, LGBT Rights Pioneer." *Advocate*, July 2, 2014. http://www.advocate.com/commentary/2014/07/02/op-ed-remembering-our-queer-history-and-wishing-happy-birthday-sylvia-rivera.

Truscott, Lucian. "Gay Power Comes to Sheridan Square." *The Village Voice*, July 3, 1969. Columbia University Libraries. http://www.columbia.edu/cu/lweb/eresources/exhibitions/sw25/voice_19690703_truscott.html.

"We all had a collective feeling like we'd had enough of this kind of shit. It wasn't anything tangible anybody said to anyone else, it was just kind of like everything over the years had come to a head on that one particular night in the one particular place, and it was not an organized demonstration. . . . Everyone in the crowd felt that we were never going to go back. It was like the last straw. It was time to reclaim something that had always been taken from us."

—Michael Fader

20.

WILDCAT

*In 1970, Postal Workers Suddenly Walked Off the Job.
The Nation, the Union, and Even President Nixon
Were Caught by Surprise*

"**W**ildcat" strikes happen when union members walk off the job despite what their leadership supports; they are usually, by definition, something uncontrollable and rather spontaneous. Wildcat strikes have been illegal in the United States since 1935, but that doesn't mean they don't still occur now and then.

The late 1960s and early 1970s saw a few of these on-the-job actions, notably the Memphis Sanitation Strike in 1968 (the folks Martin Luther King Jr. was speaking to when he was murdered) and one at Chrysler, begun by the African American–led Dodge Revolutionary Union Movement, also in 1968.

One that surprised many in the federal government was the US Postal Service's wildcat strike of 1970. On March 17 of that year, workers at National Association of Letter Carriers (NALC) Branch 36 in Manhattan, New York City, voted to strike, against the recommendations of their union leadership. Over 210,000 workers eventually walked off the job in several departments of the "post office" around the country. It's a fascinating example of union leadership not listening to the

President Nixon delivers Proclamation 3972, declaring the postal strike a national emergency

rank and file. Even more important, it demonstrated how the frustrations of regular work life for low wages could result in the kind of solidarity that is rare but encouraging.

The stated reason for the strike? Congress voted to give postal workers a 4 percent wage increase and its own members a 41 percent wage increase. It wasn't just wages, though; working conditions at the postal centers were abysmal, and these folks weren't going to take it anymore.

As the mail system ground to a halt—at a time, before the Internet, when everything from corporate checks to draft notices to census questionnaires to pretty much everything that kept the country going depended on the mail—President Nixon immediately went on national television to try to get them back to work. His words only enraged more postal workers, and 671 more locations walked out across the country. Mail was going nowhere. Workers in other government agencies also threatened to walk out in solidarity.

The strike not only completely paralyzed the US mail system, but it also affected the stock market, which suffered losses as the strike wore on; some even predicted the closure of the stock market entirely if it lasted very long.

On March 23, as post offices around the country went idle (for example, 31,000 workers walked off the job in Chicago), Nixon spoke on television once again, threatening that the National Guard would fill in for postal workers if it came to that.

This was accompanied by a proclamation from Nixon known as Proclamation 3972. It declared (or, rather, proclaimed) a "national emergency."

Nixon did, indeed, send in National Guard service members to perform some of the basic mail services in seventeen New York post offices, while at the same time negotiating with the wildcat strikers.

After eight days, the strike was over. Not one postal worker lost a job. And very soon, the National Postal Reorganization Act became law, which renamed the entity the US Postal Service and provided collective bargaining rights to the four major postal unions (National Association of Letter Carriers, American Postal Workers Union, National Postal Mail Handlers Union, and the National Rural Letter Carriers Union), including the right to negotiate on wages, benefits, and working conditions.

"For the first time these men are standing ten feet tall instead of groveling in the dust. By this action, we have graduated from an organization to a union."
—Gustave Johnson, president, NALC Branch 36

REFERENCES

Pushing the Envelope. "The 1970 Postal Strike." Smithsonian's National Postal Museum Blog. Updated March 17, 2010. http://postalmuseumblog.si.edu/2010/03/the-1970-postal-strike.html.

San Antonio Alamo Area Local #0195. "The Strike That Stunned the Country." http://saaal-apwu.org/the_strike_1970.html.

21.

ATTICA

*What Actually Happened at Attica in 1971
Is Still Largely Kept Hidden—but Clues and Facts
Are Coming Out Even Now*

The town of Attica is located on the far western side of New York. With a population of only 7,702, according to the 2010 census, there is not much around the town except for tiny rivers, hills, and woods.

In March of 1929, roughly seven hundred acres of the town were acquired for what would become Attica Correctional Facility, a prison that held roughly 2,200 inmates in 1971, mostly African American and Hispanic. The guards were all white.

The Attica Rebellion brought the plight of incarcerated individuals to the forefront of the nation's consciousness. No longer would these invisible people experience invisible injustice behind brick walls and barbed-wire fences.

One thousand of those inmates rioted and seized the prison on September 9, 1971, taking forty-two staff hostage for four days, until the state governor, Nelson Rockefeller, had the uprising quashed with six hundred state troopers and members of the National Guard, guns blazing.

As the *New York Times* reported, "The state commission that investigated the September 1971

uprising memorably described it as the bloodiest single encounter, Indian massacres aside, between Americans since the Civil War." Before it was all over:

Entrance of the Attica Correctional Facility

> Forty-three men died there, eighty-nine more were wounded. Eleven of those killed were state workers, eight guards and three civilians. All but one had been held as hostages and died in a deadly hail of friendly fire after Gov. Nelson A. Rockefeller ordered the authorities to retake the prison after a four-day standoff with mutinous inmates. One guard died two days earlier as a result of a beating inflicted by prisoners the day the riot erupted.
>
> The rest of the victims were inmates. Twenty-nine were killed by police bullets fired in the Sept. 13 retaking of the prison. Three more were executed by other inmates during the takeover for actions deemed counter to the rebellion.

What happened during and after those four days is often misrepresented by the media and by the State of New York, as well as by the prison system itself, but the real story is much more interesting. All but two of the inmates and one of the hostages who died perished at the hands of the state troopers—not the prisoners.

THE SPARK THAT LED TO REBELLION

Inmates were constantly protesting the horrid living conditions—showers once every two weeks, one roll of toilet paper a month—and rampant abuse by guards, which was especially severe for the African American and Hispanic prisoners. Political rights, like the ability to read whatever they wanted, were also a big issue. Prisoners were angry; they wrote to the Department of Corrections Commissioner Russell Oswald multiple times. They tried to get the attention of their state senator, also to no avail. Movements of the 1960s and '70s to gain rights, equality, and respect for African Americans that had begun outside the prison walls made their way into Attica and other prisons as well, so inmates began to feel empowered and able to change their daily lives in significant ways.

The people who could address the concerns of inmates at Attica remained deaf to their grievances, thinking they'd quiet down. Yet they did not quiet down—and it cost the prison, the State of New York, and the prisoners, guards, and all of their families very dearly.

THE TAKEOVER

Things came to a boil on September 9, 1971. When the guards of one cell block began to take the inmates back to their cells

"The prisoners' demands included basic civil rights such as medical care, religious and political freedom, in addition to a living wage and opportunities for education and rehabilitation."
    –The Correctional Association of New York

after breakfast rather than outside for recreation, which was the norm, the prisoners were on alert. Some reported an altercation between inmates; some say a guard harassed one inmate by keeping him in his cell rather than letting him eat, and this made his friends angry, so they stayed behind, too. Whatever it was, this small incident, in which a group of prisoners went back to their cells instead of to the yard for recreation, was the catalyst. The place exploded.

Forty-two prison guards and civilians, largely prison workers, were taken hostage, and it would be September 13 before the takeover ended—violently. During the entire four days, the self-appointed leaders of the rebellion attempted to negotiate with the state and Governor Rockefeller. It finally became clear

Screenshot from *The Nation: Attica Uprising 40 Years Later*

that the sticking point for the State of New York was amnesty from retribution when the thing was over.

THE DEMANDS

The first five demands were known as the Declaration and Five Demands of Attica. They included the following:

1. We want complete amnesty, meaning freedom from all and any physical, mental, and legal reprisals.

2. We want, now, speedy and safe transportation out of confinement to a non-imperialistic country.

3. We demand that the Federal Government intervene, so that we will be under direct Federal Jurisdiction.

4. We want the Governor and the Judiciary, namely Constance B. Motley, to guarantee that there will be no reprisals and we want all factions of the media to articulate this.

The fifth item was a list of people they wanted to come to negotiate for them, which ended with:

5. We guarantee the safe passage of all people to and from this institution. We invite all the people to come here and witness this degradation so that they can better know how to bring this degradation to an end. This is what we want.

This was expanded later to add "The Fifteen Practical Demands," asking for things such as:

•   The right to legal representation at parole hearings (which they did not have)

- A change in medical staff, to eliminate the racist and incompetent doctors working there at the time

- An end to political persecution and racial persecution

- An end to the practice of denying prisoners the right to read political newspapers and books

- The right of prisoners to form labor unions

- An end to physical and mental brutality at the hands of prison staff

- And much more, including a demand for adequate food and access to regular showers and soap

Screenshot from *The Nation: Attica Uprising 40 Years Later*

State officials knew that they wouldn't entertain the inmates' demands.

There were negotiations over all four days, but the primary sticking point for the state was the first of the five demands, which included "freedom from physical, mental, and legal reprisals." Physical, sexual, and mental abuse of prisoners was one of the primary ways the system at Attica functioned, and there was no way that eliminating reprisals would ever be accepted by the state.

On September 13, 1971, governor Nelson A. Rockefeller sent in six hundred state troopers, accompanied by air support from the National Guard. It was apparent from the start that their goal was to kill prisoners in order to "make a statement." The National Guard dropped tear gas as the troopers' guns began blazing away. In total, 4,500 rounds of ammunition were used by the state and federal militia.

The gunfire ripped apart hostages and prisoners alike. Just a few minutes later, ten hostages (mostly prison guards) and twenty-nine inmates were dead. Eighty-nine others were wounded. Before he knew about the hostages who were also shot by the militia, Governor Rockefeller called President Nixon to report that the troopers "did a fabulous job. It really was a beautiful operation." He was considerably more subdued when he found out about the "other" casualties. Especially because he knew then that his shot at the nomination for presidential candidate for the Republican Party was now scuttled.

AFTERMATH

Many stories from the prisoners were hidden or their accounts were destroyed quickly, but some are coming out now. When portions of a sealed document, *The Meyer Report*, were released in 2016, they contained several accounts of the abuse and denial of medical treatment that occurred before and after the uprising,

Screenshot from *The Nation: Attica Uprising 40 Years Later*

though a lot of key items were redacted. *The Meyer Report* has been sealed since the early 1970s, and a good deal of that information remains unavailable—for now. Much of it was documented by professor Heather Ann Thompson in the Pulitzer Prize-winning book *Blood In The Water* (Pantheon Press, 2017).

The lessons and the effects of Attica are still with us today. Professor Thompson offered the following in a phone interview in early 2016:

> There is a dual legacy from Attica. On the one hand, and after a brief moment of implementing some pretty important reforms, corrections officials used Attica to argue that prisoners needed to be clamped down on even more. And, indeed, because they told

so many lies about what had happened at Attica, many ordinary Americans bought this. But the other crucially important legacy of Attica was that prisoners never stopped resisting that kind of draconian treatment.

Frankly, what Attica shows is that there's a very long history of covering up for police misconduct. And that misconduct includes the abuse and killing of our nation's most disenfranchised and marginalized citizens. It also speaks to the lengths that officials will go to not take responsibility for their actions.

When incidents in Ferguson and Baltimore and other, similar brutal police actions end in the deaths of African Americans, and the official story is immediately changed until nobody really knows what happened, that's one method of obfuscation that officials learned in Attica: cover-ups make it easier to obscure the truth.

We can only hope that other, forward-looking lessons will emerge in the area of prison reform, as we confront the fact that the United States incarcerates more people than the entire rest of the world combined. The systemic racism and abuse by the prison state and its machinery demand much more outrage and action from the American people in order for things to change.

REFERENCES

Associated Press. "Attica Prison report reveals inmates beaten, tortured." *Al Jazeera America*, May 22, 2015. http://america.aljazeera.com/articles/2015/5/22/new-report-on-attica-prison-riot-reveals-inmates-were-beaten.html.

"The Attica Prison Uprising: Forty Years Later." YouTube, March 29, 2012. https://www.youtube.com/watch?v=cBG1UkxrMG0.

The Correctional Association of New York. "Attica Correctional Factility: 2011—Basic Facts, Findings & Recommendations." http://www.correctionalassociation.org/wp-content/uploads/2012/05/Attica2011FactSheet.pdf.

History.com. "Riot at Attica Prison." This Day in History, 2010. http://www.history.com/this-day-in-history/riot-at-attica-prison.

Robbins, Tom. "A Brutal Beating Wakes Attica's Ghosts." *New York Times*, February 28, 2015. https://www.nytimes.com/2015/03/01/nyregion/attica-prison-infamous-for-bloodshed-faces-a-reckoning-as-guards-go-on-trial.html.

Roberts, Sam. "Rockefeller on the Attica Raid, From Boastful to Subdued." *New York Times*, September 12, 2011. http://www.nytimes.com/2011/09/13/nyregion/rockefeller-initially-boasted-to-nixon-about-attica-raid.html.

Schuessler, Jennifer. "Prying Loose the Long-Kept Secrets of Attica." *New York Times*, August 23, 2016. https://www.nytimes.com/2016/08/24/books/prying-loose-the-long-kept-secrets-of-attica.html.

**Screen shot from *The Nation:*
*The Attica Uprising 40 Years Later***

Thompson, Heather Ann. "The Attica Uprising." *Against the Current* 126
    (2007). https://solidarity-us.org/node/313.

Thompson, Heather Ann. "Empire State Disgrace: The Dark, Secret History
    of the Attica Prison Tragedy." *Salon*, October 25, 2014.
    http://www.salon.com/2014/05/25/empire_state_disgrace_the_dark
    _secret_history_of_the_attica_prison_tragedy/.

Thompson, Heather Ann. "How Attica's Ugly Past Is Still Protected." *Time*,
    May 26, 2015. http://time.com/3896825/attica-1971-meyer-report
    -release/.

22.

THE WATSONVILLE, CALIFORNIA, CANNERY STRIKE

This Is What Solidarity Looks Like

n the mid-1980s, the US labor movement was very much on its heels after four years of Reaganism and its accompanying attacks on labor unions, beginning with the air traffic controllers' strike of 1981: Reagan ordered that all the striking controllers be fired and destroyed their union.

In this atmosphere, more than a thousand largely Latina workers showed a bright spark of fight-back with the 1985–1987 Watsonville Cannery strike, which saw absolutely none of the workers crossing the picket line until the strike was settled. It taxed the local community in unexpected ways, as food and other resources were used up, strike pay ended, and unemployment benefits ceased, but the resolve of the cannery workers remained unbroken until a favorable contract was reached.

The two thousand Latina workers at the two companies involved, Watsonville Canning and Richard A. Shaw Frozen Foods, struck on September 7, 1985. During contract negotiations with International Brotherhood of Teamsters Local 912, the companies had sought a 30 percent reduction in base pay and benefits such as vacation time and seniority—severely impacting the women who had worked at these companies for decades. The same things were happening across the industry, and several other unionized plants had already agreed to wage and benefit reductions.

Known as the "Frozen Vegetable Capital of the World" prior to the strike, Watsonville's population was made up largely of Latina workers from the surrounding factories and warehouses. This actually aided in keeping the solidarity necessary to survive the strike, and everyone knew it. It also meant that community support was deep, since everyone who lived in the area either had worked there or was related to people who did.

IT TAKES A VILLAGE

The walkout began September 7. Because strike benefits were 20 percent of peak wages, the women immediately began to plan and combine resources—sharing housing and food, childcare, and more. Many strikers were single mothers, so in a sense, some of these community-building resources were things they were accustomed to already. They just had to push it to extremes.

In addition, some financial help was provided by the United Farm Workers (UFW) as well as Latino-focused organizations such as the League Of United Latin American Citizens and the Mexican American Political Association. Local grocery stores extended credit to the strikers, and some even refused to cash the paychecks brought in by "replacement workers," or scabs.

Images from *Watsonville On Strike*

From the start, the companies involved tried to hire scabs to perform the work. But as anyone who's ever spent time in a factory can attest, they couldn't do the job—and most certainly wouldn't do it for long, given the low wages, lack of benefits, betrayal of the local community, and unlikelihood of still being on the job when it was all over. As Frank Bardacke details in *The Workers, United*:

> A new recruit can become an average broccoli trimmer in a couple of weeks, among an experienced crew ready both to teach and to cover for a beginner's mistakes. Just moving your hands skillfully is only part of the job. What's tough is standing on the hard wet concrete for twelve-hour shifts, with the deafening noise, the endless movement of the product on the belt, the pressure from the floorladies and the chicken-shit company rules.
>
> All that is bad for $6.66 an hour plus medical benefits and a week's paid vacation. But when you have to be bused in with police escorts, or return to the parking lot and find your car with four punctured tires, and when you make only $5.05 an hour with no benefits and no job security, the job becomes a poor deal indeed.

Like almost all clashes between working people and the ruling class, the local police were used to try and intimidate strikers—sometimes with violence, sometimes with fear, and always on the side of the owners. As one striker said in the documentary *Watsonville On Strike*, "The police want to scare us . . . [they] are sold out to our boss."

After just six months, the local union at Shaw Frozen Foods ratified a contract that included a somewhat less severe pay cut. This came after the Shaw owners showed their ailing financials

"Just because you're Catholic doesn't mean you can't throw rocks at scabs."
–Gloria Betancourt, striker, in *Jacobin* magazine.

to the union, which Watsonville Canning refused to do. Watsonville Canning strikers were temporarily disheartened by this and by watching other canneries around them close down and move to Mexico and Central America. But they kept on going.

And they watched as their fellow workers lost homes, cars, and sometimes their entire families, as marriages suffered and some people just picked up and moved away. Yet, the strikers stood even more unified and helped their sisters and brothers make it through another day.

Another full year later, Watsonville Canning's main bank, Wells Fargo, withdrew its line of credit not just because it feared the cannery would not survive but also because the Teamsters International union was preparing to withdraw $800 million in investments from the rapidly growing bank.

Now bankrupt, Watsonville Canning was taken over by new owners, and what initially looked like a break in the strike—a contract negotiated with the new owners by Teamsters Local 912—felt like another slap in the face: no improvement in the wage cuts and a removal of health benefits. Despite the urgings of all but one of the local union officials who negotiated that contract, the women voted against it again and went out on a "wildcat" strike, which is an action that is not approved of or sanctioned by local union officers, who had declared the strike over. But these workers had not endured almost two years of struggle just to accept another shoddy deal that left them in poverty.

THE PEREGRINACIÓN

Anger at being sold out again turned into action. The strikers envisioned and then organized and put into action a *peregrinación*, or pilgrimage, wherein they crawled on their knees from the cannery to the nearest Catholic church, a distance of

"What made the critical difference was the strikers themselves—not just their tenacity and determination but their readiness, at crucial points, to take the initiative, assume responsibility, and make and carry out key strategic decisions."
    —Peter Shapiro, activist and author of *The Song of the Stubborn 1,000*

over a mile. Their union sisters placed blankets under their knees as they crawled on the cement, and then picked up those blankets and moved them to the front as the participants neared the edge of the next blanket. This took place with banners and images of Jesus, Mary, and the saints held high. It was a variation on the tactic successfully used by the United Farm Workers more than fifteen years before.

The procession moved all who saw it to tears. As they arrived at the Catholic church, where the new company owners and the attorneys representing them worshipped every Sunday, there was no way to deny the strikers what they deserved. The company agreed to reinstate their health benefits, and the strike was over.

In an interview with a maintenance man from the plant who refused to go back until the strike was settled—despite earning much less working part time somewhere else—author Frank Bardacke captured the essence of how the solidarity of these workers remained intact. Said the worker:

> There is no way for a striker to cross that picket line and live in Watsonville . . . I don't think anybody would hurt me. But I couldn't go anywhere in town with my head up, on the chance that I might have to look some striker in the eye. I couldn't come to this Y[MCA], I couldn't shop at the grocery store, I couldn't go to the bingo game. For the rest of my life I would be the mechanic who betrayed my people. No money is worth that. I will go back to work Watsonville Canning with everybody else or not all.

It was this solidarity—in the face of attacks from the companies, the police, and sometimes their own union representatives—that got the workers through it.

REFERENCES

Bardacke, Frank. "The Workers United." *El Andar* (October 1995). http://www.elandar.com/back/www-oct95/andar/cover/cannery.htm.

Corwin, Miles. "Canning Workers' Bitter Strike Devastates Lives, Economy of Watsonville." *Los Angeles Times*, September 14, 1986. http://articles.latimes.com/1986-09-14/news/mn-12455_1_production-workers.

McCartin, Joseph A. "The Strike That Busted Unions." *New York Times*, August 2, 2011. http://www.nytimes.com/2011/08/03/opinion/reagan-vs-patco-the-strike-that-busted-unions.html.

Shapiro, Peter. "Nothing to Lose." *Jacobin*, November 2, 2016. https://www.jacobinmag.com/2016/11/watsonville-canning-strike-women-strikebreakers.

Shapiro, Peter. *Song of the Stubborn One Thousand: The Watsonville Canning Strike, 1985–87.* Chicago: Haymarket Books, 2016.

Suárez-Orozco, Marcelo and Mariela Páez. *Latinos: Remaking America.* Oakland: University of California Press, 2008.

"Watsonville Canning Strike." St. James Encyclopedia of Labor History Worldwide: Major Events in Labor History and Their Impact. September 19, 2017. http://www.encyclopedia.com/history/encyclopedias-almanacs-transcripts-and-maps/watsonville-canning-strike.

"Watsonville On Strike—excerpt." YouTube, January 3, 2017. https://www.youtube.com/watch?v=tcSPSanxM8M.

Images of the peregrinación and the celebration of the strike settlement via Remembering the Struggle

23.

UPS

*Those Packages Won't Move Themselves:
Big Brown Versus the IBT*

I t's fair to say that United Parcel Service (UPS) rolled the dice in 1997, thinking the International Brotherhood of Teamsters union wasn't "in the game" enough to fight hard when the company was preparing for contract negotiations that year. The union had been divided by internal political battles for quite a while, and it had staged an unsuccessful, rather disorganized one-day strike three years previous, which had led to the union being sued by UPS. Its strike fund was nearly broke, too.

What greeted the company in 1997, however, was militance, workers' solidarity, muscle, and intense rank-and-file action that united the UPS workforce around just a few key issues: part-time workers, wages, and the pensions that the men and women dressed in brown had worked for all their lives.

Beginning in the 1970s, UPS had begun moving a lot of its full-time workforce to part-time. Also, in 1982, it had cut wages for part-timers by more than a third, down to eight dollars an hour. Heading into contract negotiations in 1996, these remained the key issues for members. Contract surveys that went out prior to the start of negotiations that year made clear that two out of three workers at UPS were considered part-time, with accompanying reduced pay and benefits. Further, 90 percent of the survey respondents who were classified as part-time stated that full-time work with full-time pay was their highest priority.

In addition to the pre-negotiation surveys of UPS Teamster members, pre-strike rallies were held to build momentum, and a petition signed by active employees reached 100,000 signatures—out of a workforce of 185,000. The union also set up phone hotlines and even a dedicated website (if that doesn't sound like a big thing, remember this was during a time when that wasn't so common, pre-Facebook and all.)

Some of the preparation might have seemed excessive. For example, a rally in Chicago, held four days before contract negotiations began, featured two representatives from every one of the 206 Teamster local unions in the country that had UPS members flying in to participate. That spirit continued in the weeks to follow, as rallies held at local worksites began to fire up all over the country. For the first time ever, all shop stewards nationwide received a seven-minute video on the status of contract negotiations. Stickers began to appear on brown UPS uniforms that stated, "It's Our Contract. We'll Fight for It." This was deep, thoughtful preparation.

Negotiations weren't getting anywhere in mid-July, and the union held a strike authorization vote; 95 percent of the membership approved.

UPS presented its final offer, which included no changes to wages or the treatment of part-time workers, and it also pushed to get the company out of the Teamster joint pension plan, which would hurt future retirees. On August 4, 1997, the union members walked off the job.

In sheer numbers, this was the largest strike the country had seen yet; 185,000 people were fighting UPS by not showing up that day, and very close to 100 percent joined the walkout.

Teamsters rally during the 1997 UPS strike

This was absolutely not expected by UPS, which was hoping that tens of thousands would cross the picket lines and work as scabs.

With any service-oriented company such as UPS, the customers are as key to the operation as the workers themselves. The union members who drove the routes every day and handled the packages knew this, so they arranged to meet regular customers along their routes during the strike to let them know why they walked out and what progress was being made. The Teamsters union even passed out pro-union "baseball cards" at ball games to build community support.

Such a large number of workers on strike requires a robust strike fund, which the Teamsters did not have on hand; other unions and the AFL-CIO in Washington loaned them the money to keep paying those bills while the strike went on.

Three days before the end of the strike was negotiated, the Teamsters union called for a nationwide "day of action" that involved union members from across all walks of life. This helped build even more community and public support for the workers engaged in such a front-and-center battle with a company that represented all that was wrong with corporate America.

UPS appealed to president Bill Clinton to intervene, claiming the massive shipping outage caused by the strike was interfering with the nation's commerce. Clinton declined, though near the end of the strike, he did send some of his best mediators to help break down the walls.

Not expecting such a solid rank-and-file effort led by a union that seemed on the rocks, UPS accepted most of the union's demands when the final contract was settled and the members ratified it on August 20, 1997. Ten thousand part-time jobs would be moved to full-time, ten thousand new full-time hires would come on board, the largest wage increases in UPS history were

Logo from Teamsters Local 952. Used with permission

Image via YouTube, "America's Victory: The 1997 UPS Strike"

implemented, and the company would remain in the joint employer pension fund. But what UPS also did not expect was the dramatic hemorrhaging of cash it sustained; it estimated $600 million in losses during a two-week strike, which in 2017 dollars is over $1 billion. No company can keep that going for long.

During a time when unions were losing public relations battles and especially members, the 1997 UPS Teamster strike stands as one of the most successful battles with a massive corporation in decades, and it shows what solidarity and good old-fashioned smart organizing can do.

REFERENCES

"America's Victory: The 1997 UPS Strike." YouTube, July 27, 2007. https://www.youtube.com /watch?v=NbYqoGM0GX8&feature=youtu.be.

Herbert, Bob. "A Workers' Rebellion." *New York Times*, August 7, 1997. http://www.nytimes.com /1997/08/07/opinion/a-workers-rebellion.html.

Greenhouse, Steven. "Yearlong Effort Key to Success for Teamsters." *New York Times*, August 25, 1997. http://www.nytimes.com/1997/08/25/us /yearlong-effort-key-to-success-for-teamsters .html.

"It's Official: Teamsters End UPS Strike." *CNN*, August 20, 1997. http://www.cnn.com /US/9708/20/ups.update.early/.

"More than 10,000 part-timers are working 35 or more hours a week, and they continue to be paid as part-timers. In the corporate suites, that is called smart management. In other places, it is called ripping people off.

It is more a rebellion than a strike. The walkout by 185,000 drivers, loaders and sorters of the United Parcel Service is best seen as the angry, fist-waving response of the frustrated American worker, a revolt against the ruthless treatment of workers by so many powerful corporations."

–Bob Herbert, *New York Times,* August 7, 1997

24.

THE FIGHT FOR $15

The Long Game, and Why It's Part of Labor's Future

One of the most important battles being waged today among working people is the fight to raise the minimum wage. Being in a union on the job generally means earning a higher rate than minimum wage (the current federal minimum wage as of this writing is $7.25 an hour, though some states actually peg it lower), but organizing fast food, retail, and other minimum-wage workers into a union is a challenging prospect, indeed. Some of the reasons why: it's frequently transient work; those who labor in these places are usually too scared/tired/broke to want to get involved; and there's a ton of money allied against the efforts to organize these workers by the fast food franchises and retail giants and the associations that represent them.

One union that has taken that challenge head-on is the Service Employees International Union (SEIU).

The movement began around 2012, originally with multiple entities in different cities, known as Fast Food Forward, Raise Up MKE (Milwaukee), Stand Up KC (Kansas City), Low Pay Is Not OK, and more. All of these merged into Fight For $15 in 2015.

It created a groundswell that has staged one-day strikes all around the country, and the movement

Workers rally at a Fight for $15 protest

claims as victories cities such as Seattle, Los Angeles, and San Francisco, as well as New York State, that have passed legislation to increase the minimum wage to $15 an hour over several years.

Workers who are forced to live on the kinds of wages that pay $7.25 an hour or less (servers and some others at table-service restaurants, for example, work for as little as $2.13 per hour before tips, depending on which state they work in) often depend on public assistance for survival—food stamps, Medicaid, and more. As these programs are made inaccessible due to budget cuts and other attacks on the poor—inevitable during Republican administrations in Washington—the desperation that follows might just spark even more rallies, organizing drives, and walkouts.

The stakes are high; if the SEIU can negotiate a contract with a company as large as, say, McDonald's, then many more workforces would likely follow suit across this industry in other industries—food service, hotel workers, chain auto repair shops, and so many more.

An SEIU victory could also be significant for the future of organized labor; these are some of the folks usually left behind in traditional unionizing efforts, and many of them are African American, Latino, or other people of color. The rallying cry has changed, too. From simply the fight for $15 an hour to both *$15 and a union* represents a key difference.

The returns for the labor movement are high-stakes. With unionization across the United States at historically low rates (in 2016, 6.4 percent of private sector and 34.4 percent of public sector workers were union members), this is a way for unions to show their power, expose new generations of people to what unions are about, and maybe—just maybe —demonstrate what solidarity means.

Given the political climate since the 2016 election, the very lives and economic futures of a significant part of the working poor will depend on movements like Fight For $15 and their success.

The old IWW slogan of "An Injury to One Is an Injury to All" applies here: if multinational corporations making massive profits can get away with treating these workers so very poorly, then the rest of us must feel it, as well, and respond accordingly. Even if it means we can't go and get that burger for lunch because they're picketing today.

If you're like me, you'll join them in walking the lines, picket sign in hand, fighting for $15.

"I've never in my thirty-two years in the labor movement seen anything like this before."
—Mary Kay Henry, president, SEIU

REFERENCES

Bureau of Labor Statistics. "Union Members Summary." Last modified January 26, 2017. https://www.bls.gov/news.release/union2.nr0.htm.

Greenhouse, Steven. "How to Get Low Wage Workers Into the Middle Class." *Atlantic*, August 19, 2015. https://www.theatlantic.com/business/archive/2015/08/fifteen-dollars-minimum-wage/401540/.

Gupta, Arun. "Fight for $15 Confidential." *In These Times*, November 11, 2013. http://inthesetimes.com/article/15826/fight_for_15_confidential.

Luckerson, Victor. "Here's Every City in America Getting a $15 Minimum Wage." *Time*, July 23, 2015. http://time.com/3969977/minimum-wage/.

Parti, Tarini. "Fast Food Strike Takes Over 60 Cities." *Politico*, August 29, 2013. http://www.politico.com/story/2013/08/fast-food-strike-096032.

SEIU members rally at a Fight for $15 protest

25.

WOODY GUTHRIE

Why Several Verses of "This Land Is Your Land"
Are Usually Left Off When It's Taught in School

Woodrow Wilson "Woody" Guthrie was a poet, songwriter, and musician who often traveled with a sticker or two on his guitar that read, "This Machine Kills Fascists."

Guthrie wrote a massive collection of political, folk, and children's songs during his relatively short life (some of which are referenced in chapters of this book), and ever since, versions of many of them have been performed and recorded by musicians from Johnny Cash to Bob Dylan to Billy Bragg to Bruce Springsteen to Ani DiFranco.

The most popular of his songs is one that almost every schoolkid in the United States knows at least in part. It's an easy-to-learn piece entitled, "This Land Is Your Land":

> *This land is your land, this land is my land*
> *From California to the New York island;*
> *From the redwood forest to the Gulf Stream waters*
> *This land was made for you and me.*
>
> *As I was walking that ribbon of highway,*
> *I saw above me that endless skyway:*

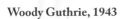

I saw below me that golden valley:
This land was made for you and me.

Those are probably the two verses that are most often taught in grade school music classes all across this land. A few of those lines were even sung during the halftime show at the 2017 NFL Super Bowl—by none other than Lady Gaga.

But there are a few more verses of this particular song that tend to get . . . ahem, shuffled off into history:

I've roamed and rambled and I followed my footsteps
To the sparkling sands of her diamond deserts;
And all around me a voice was sounding:
This land was made for you and me.

When the sun came shining, and I was strolling,
And the wheat fields waving and the dust clouds rolling,
As the fog was lifting a voice was chanting:
This land was made for you and me.

"OK, Weber," I can almost hear you thinking. "There's nothing all that controversial about those words. What kinda hype are you selling us here?" Wait for it:

As I went walking I saw a sign there
And on the sign it said "No Trespassing."
But on the other side it didn't say nothing,
That side was made for you and me.

In the shadow of the steeple I saw my people,
By the relief office I seen my people;
As they stood there hungry, I stood there asking
Is this land made for you and me?

Nobody living can ever stop me,
As I go walking that freedom highway;

Nobody living can ever make me turn back
This land was made for you and me.

The "other side" of that sign meant for you and me—and the hungry people standing in the "relief" (food donation) lines—that's the kind of thing that leads to people challenging the status quo, and to union organizing drives, and to people fighting back, and to being mad as hell and not willing to take it anymore. This land? It might be "Made for you and me," but there are powerful people who are trying to take it—all of it—away from us.

If we have learned anything from these stories of union members, veterans, prisoners, and simple, common, hard-working men and women fighting back, I hope it's this: We can win. Sometimes, that victory might take a number of battles. It might take years. It might mean the loss of some of our people along the way, and of other things very important to us as the battles rage on.

It will take an alliance of nearly everyone: working people, veterans, farmers, immigrants, environmentalists, the unemployed, and probably some politicians worth their salt as well, uniting in a class war—one that we didn't ask for, but that we have to wage, regardless—in order to wrest from the 1 percent what is rightfully ours.

But we must fight. And we will win.

INDEX

ABOUT THE AUTHOR

Steve Schlicht

BRANDON WEBER has written for the *Progressive*, *Upworthy*, *Big Think*, *Common Dreams*, *Liberals Unite*, and many other publications. He has been a union activist for more than thirty years. He lives in Michigan.

WILL FISCHER is the director of government relations for VoteVets, the largest progressive veterans' organization in America. Previously, he spent nearly a decade working at the AFL-CIO, and his commentary has been featured on MSNBC, CNN, Fox News, and in hundreds of magazines and newspapers.